Testing Positive

365 Days of Calm Through Chaos

Written by
Sylvia Marusyk

ISBN: 9798848711080

Cover Design: Sean Ferstl

Praise for *Testing Positive: 365 Days of Calm Through Chaos*

"To take a tragedy and turn it to a triumph takes strength, wisdom, and spiritual insight. Sylvia turned the words 'testing positive' into a life of grace and gratitude where she chose to share those gifts with the world through her work. As a fellow cancer thriver, I resonate deeply with the awareness and lifestyle she embraces and the desire to serve others to overcome barriers. No matter what journey you're facing in life, the golden nuggets of hope she provides within each page will enrich your day. What a beautiful triumph that we get to share and co-create in her thought-provoking heart-work." ~ Jenny Mulks, Cancer Wellness Coach - Circle of Hope Cancer Support
Founder & CEO - Along Comes Hope®

"Sylvia Marusyk is the ultimate thriver, and her message in *Testing Positive: 365 Days of Calm Through Chaos* will guide you on your own thriving journey. On the first page the reader will absorb her powerful, positive, and victorious energy. Thrust into a battle for her life, oh how easy would it have been to cave, and latch on to the victim mindset. 'Why me?' quickly becomes 'Why not me?' She exemplifies walking the walk, showing others how to live through a life fiercely challenged. Using her inspiration, you will emerge the hero in your own journey!" ~ Bruce Pulver, Global TedX Speaker, and author of *Above The Chatter, Our Words Matter.*

When I first met Sylvia I felt a certain energy and spark that always left me feeling positive and good. She has a way of looking at things and making the most of it, even with her own battle with cancer. I am thrilled Sylvia is now sharing her story and knowledge with the rest of the world, a thought provoking read if you are *Testing Positive*, but Sylvia will show you how to make *365 Days of Calm Through Chaos,* towards a more fulfilling and happier life. ~ Tracy Koga, Creator and Founder of Hue Productions, ilikehue.com.

"If you have ever doubted that you are up to life's challenges, Sylvia Marusyk's new book, *Testing Positive: 365 Days of Calm Through Chaos,* is a must-read! Begin with her powerful introduction—that will likely do the trick. But don't stop there. Every page contains enough energy to launch you into battle!"
~ Mark Hardcastle, Airline Captain, Speaker, Writer, Trainer, and Author of *The Symphony of Your Life: Restoring Harmony When Your World Is Out of Tune.*

Dedication

To my children, Nathaniel and Elyssia Yaeger. You are my heart beats, and the reason for everything I do. And to David, you are my home and refuge.

Introduction

December 17, 2019.

She made that face. You know the one; the expression that says, "Oh no, this is not good." She tried to hide it, but you can't mask that face.

"She" was the individual doing my annual mammogram. I appreciated her attempt to soften the blow, but I prefer to face things head on. "You found something, didn't you?" She glanced at me, then back at the x-ray. "Well, I just need another picture. Maybe a better view." Code for "Yes, but I can't say anything." She was stalling. More pain, the worst pain I've ever had with a mammogram. That pretty much confirmed it for me. I was taken back to the waiting room and told I would need an ultrasound.

After the ultrasound, I received the news. There was something there. The doctor was concerned, so she sent a referral for an immediate biopsy. A solitary tear slipped from my right eye. She offered me a tissue, but I said, "No thank you, I'm good. I'll handle whatever this." Brave words, but I meant every one.

Of all days, the biopsy was scheduled for Christmas Eve. Merry freaking Christmas! Not gonna lie, I felt pretty sorry for myself. Especially on Christmas morning when I took the bandages off. I was horrified! It looked as though someone had repeatedly kicked me in my left breast. I was black and blue! I needed to think, and somehow process what was happening. It was freezing outside, but I had to move. I grabbed my coat and headed for the door. I often went for walks by myself, but that day I actually felt alone. I cried, screamed, and swore. How could this be happening to me? I was ashamed of my weakness for being scared but told myself to feel it all. It was just me and fear, battling for control of my mind and emotions. I wouldn't run from it or try to bury my feelings. I would look it straight in the eye and make damn sure it blinked first. I won't pretend it was easy. I was literally fighting for my life, and there were moments when I wanted to give in, but I held on to hope and to the knowledge that I could choose how to face the situation. By the time I arrived home after my walk, I had exorcised most of the darkness and fear that had gripped my soul. I did, in fact, have a merry Christmas.

On January 3, 2020, I received a call from my doctor's office letting me know the biopsy results were in. I already had an appointment on January 7 with a surgeon, but my doctor asked if I wanted to review the results earlier. No way I was going to wait, so my daughter and I went to the office that afternoon. The diagnosis wasn't good. Invasive ductal carcinoma. I was stunned. My doctor wasn't usually a woman of animation and expression, but that day she looked very sad and said, "I'm so sorry. You've been through so much these last few years." I actually wanted to comfort her! As my daughter and I left, we talked about the reality of what was to come. We both knew and spoke out loud the fact that we were going to get through all of it, and that I would be okay.

That evening I went to the wedding of a friend. I wore the hottest red dress I had, full of sparkles and sequins, and got totally glammed up. I had the best time and was able to let everything go for a while.

The following week I went to my appointment with the surgeon, where she repeated the diagnosis I'd been given days before. My family history had caught up with me. The first question she asked was whether or not I was going to have a mastectomy. In my mind I was thinking, *What the hell?! Is this actually a menu item? Is this actually being considered?*

Finally, I managed to ask what I thought would be an obvious question with a clear answer. "Could I just have the lump removed?" She went on to explain that the type of cancer I was diagnosed with carried a lifetime risk, never going into full remission, and that some women opt for a mastectomy right off the bat. I tried to get my head around the news, but it felt like I was on the outside looking in. It was like I was watching a movie and it was all happening to someone else. How could it be? I mean, I wasn't sick! I was the healthy one. I was the one who would never get the cancer that ran in my family. I did everything right, yet there I was informing a surgeon of my decision to get a lumpectomy. It was beyond surreal.

We went back home and my son came over. We all sat together and talked about what was happening. It was a rough night. At one point, my son seemed emotional and I said to him, "Honey, you know I'm going to be okay, right?" He nodded. "Yeah, I just don't want you to think you can green smoothie and meditate this away. You have to listen to the doctors." I reassured him that I wouldn't make any decisions without consulting him and his sister, my doctors, as well as my own body. I also gently assured him I'd adopt a blend of naturopathic and western medicine for the best possible outcome.

I was used to not sleeping well, but that night was far worse. Getting up the next morning was rough, but I had to go to work. I knew I'd have to work as much as possible before my surgery, because I'd be out of work for a while afterwards without medical leave insurance. I left home and went to a factory where I had been providing injury prevention services for the last ten years. I was there for three hours, working with injured workers and people struggling with life issues. They were my people, and the work my passion. When the day was finished, I climbed into my car and looked at myself in the rear-view mirror. It struck me that, for the three hours I was working in the factory, not one thought about myself or my situation had entered my mind. Helping and serving others is some powerful medicine! I kept looking at myself in the mirror and said out loud, "F**k cancer! If you can make a difference in people's lives while dealing with this disease, you are unstoppable! Nothing will stop you. This will be nothing in your life. Your purpose is much bigger, and don't you forget that!" The time I spent working in that factory had been priceless therapy and it changed the game in my favor.

My surgery was scheduled for February 24, 2020. I was convinced it would be life-changing in so many ways. As a woman, I knew it would affect my self-image, but I also believed it would help me unload the grief, heartbreak, fear, and anger I felt were locked up in my breast (the left breast is the maternal breast) from everything I'd gone through in previous years. I had been working on that with my body talk therapist and believed I'd made excellent progress. I felt like all of the stuff that was bottled up inside of me had moved from my heart into the small tumor. Once the tumor was removed, I'd be done with that. Ah, but nothing is quite that simple though, is it? While all of that was going on, I also had the nagging feeling that I had been a fraud to my audiences for the past twenty years. After all, I was the person telling everyone they could create health instead of disease. I was the one proclaiming, "Your issues live in your tissues, so deal with your issues before they become symptoms, illness, and disease. I can teach you how!" And what happened to me? Apparently, my issues found a home in my tissues, and I became someone with a disease.

I don't believe in coincidences. I never have. A low-flying angel, and friend, changed everything for me with one brief text message. I have no doubt she was sent to deliver this message to me: "Sylvia, you have spent the last many years in training for this exact moment in time. You will win, and this will become part of your amazing story!" In the depths of my soul, I knew her message was true. I knew the disease would be a gateway to something bigger, and that I would be okay!

Did I mention I also had knee surgery five days before my breast surgery? That's right, two surgeries back-to-back. Some would say that's a bit crazy, not to mention hard on the body, but I intuitively knew it was the right thing to do. It would allow me to work as much as possible and take less time off. Rather than trying to schedule recovery time for two surgeries, it would essentially be one block of time off for both. It seemed like a great plan, and it worked out perfectly. An interesting thing happened during that time. Pain and I are not friends. In fact, you might say I have a severe allergy to pain. Like, I'm terrified of it! Yet, for both surgeries I was calm and relaxed, and not just mentally. All of my vitals were monitored during the procedures, and they showed I was also at peace physically. I had no fear and knew that everything would be fine. I didn't know how they were going to remove the tumor, where they would cut to access it, and I never asked, prior to the moments before going in to the OR. I did everything possible to not buy into the notion that I was ill or had a condition of any kind. When the resident spoke with me before the surgery and shared with me their plan, I just thought, *Okay. Do whatever you need to do.* I wished they could make the scar as invisible as possible. But that was not the case, they did what they had to do and I'm learning to love my scar. It's a symbol of my survival and resilience.

Five days later I was presenting for one of my favorite clients, the Canadian Canola Growers Association. A few days after that I was on stage at a local hotel and speaking to hundreds of people in the aviation industry. I was in my happy place!

Just as I was recovering and getting back into my life, COVID-19 hit. Everything on my schedule was canceled. All of my conferences, and along with it, all of my income sources. Even the conferences I had scheduled for the latter part of 2020 were canceled. It was all very concerning, but the gift in the situation was the abundance of extra time I was given to work on something else. Even though the tumor had been removed from my body, I still felt as though something was holding me back. I couldn't quite put a finger on it, and I can only describe the feeling as "sticky." I needed time to dig deep into it, and I was given that time.

I had an intense dream one night that woke me up in a cold sweat. I was in a room full of friends and we were all happy and talking. Everything was fine, when suddenly I began choking and gagging. I started vomiting and hit the floor on all fours. Black smoke poured out of my mouth and filled the room, and then I lost consciousness. When I awoke from the dream it felt like I had been completely transformed. It was an energetic release of epic proportions, and the darkness that had lived in me for so long was gone. I felt so light and free. And yet, there was something still lurking just beneath the surface.

During that time, another low-flying angel delivered a perfectly timed message. Theo Heineman, a good friend, mentor, and spiritual sister, reconnected with me and we started spending time together. One day, she began talking about how our stories from childhood affect us. She is one of only a few dozen people worldwide who are trained to deliver the work of Joe Dispenza. She reminded me of his work and we talked about it at length. I realized that this was somehow a key to whatever it was that was "sticky," and whatever lingered in my maternal breast even after the tumor was removed, and the inner work I'd done up to that point. It took three days of deep meditation to unearth what the stickiness was. I asked three mornings in a row, "What is the teaching of this disease? What am I supposed to do with this? How is this going to serve me and others?" Crickets for three days, but I finally received the word. The meaning of the disease? My powerlessness. My lifelong submission to people of authority, or people I perceived to have authority. It was my childhood story that I brought into my adult life.

My father was a viciously abusive man. Physically, verbally, and emotionally. As a child, all I really wanted to do was protect my mother. It doesn't take long for a child to realize they have no control or power in those situations, so I became as perfect as possible so I wouldn't be the cause of my father's anger. He would take his anger out on any of us, so I thought I could distract him with my goodness. Maybe if I got straight A's and was helpful, he wouldn't get angry. That was the story I'd formed in my mind. I carried that desire to please, to be submissive and not ruffle feathers, into adulthood. Couple that with the fact that I belonged to a very conservative, patriarchal church, and the scene was set. All my life I had attracted people who would validate my powerlessness. I would give my power away and perpetuate my childhood story. To say I was a people-pleaser would be an understatement, and it's no surprise that my own archetype is that of a nurturer. I've always excelled at whatever I decided to dive into, so I became excellent at nurturing. No matter the situation, I attracted people who would keep me in my powerless state. Coworkers, bosses, friends, and even family members.

Once I uncovered that lie in meditation, I realized that a powerless person cannot fight cancer. The time had come for me to step into my power. Isn't it amazing, when you experience such revelations and realizations, how God or the Universe delivers? I had an opportunity the very next day to show up for myself in a way I never had before. I felt a little anxious but felt my power and ability to rise to the challenge even more. Sometimes, you don't realize how bad you've been feeling until you suddenly feel great! I had finally exposed the lie that had governed and oppressed me my entire life, and the feeling was indescribable. For the first time in my life I tasted genuine freedom, and knew I'd never go back. As you know, the mind and body are connected, so as I dealt with all of those things, my body reacted with infections—just more s**t that needed to be released along with powerlessness. That went on for a month! There were some tough moments in there, but I sailed through them knowing exactly what the outcome was going to be. I was going to be okay. In fact, I was going to be fantastic!

Radiation was something I was not looking forward to, but had decided, based on my research, to go ahead with. I personally did not want chemotherapy and I am so blessed that test results indicated it wasn't necessary. The original recommendation was five weeks of radiation, every day except on the weekends. How was I going to do that? Logistically, I had no choice but to work (little did I know that travel and in fact work, would be suspended indefinitely due to the pandemic) and you cannot travel when you're undergoing radiation. Plus, there's the potential side effects of extreme fatigue, blistering skin etc. As it turned out, at least I didn't need to worry about cancelling any travel, it was done for me! My body kept telling me it didn't want five weeks of radiation. It was saying it really couldn't be more than three.

My first trip to the cancer care center was tough. I went alone, and memories of me taking my brother to the same place back in 2008 for treatments flooded my mind. It was an emotional time, but I was determined to be strong and knew I could be. As I sat in the room waiting for the radiation oncologist to come in, I spoke these words to myself out loud, "You're okay. You're okay. Your anxiety is not based on anything real. You know nothing yet so be calm and breathe." The resident came into the room first and told me that the plan was for five weeks of radiation. Soon after, when the radiation oncologist entered, he said, "I'm going to suggest three weeks of radiation." I told him I thought that was wonderful, and that my body really didn't want more than three weeks. I had even been telling my friends that three weeks was all I was doing. I think he understood. How amazing was that though? Things got easier after the first appointment, because I realized I wasn't sick! I never once thought of myself as someone who had cancer, and I never will. That mindset made everything better.

By early April, the infections were finally healed, and it was time to schedule radiation treatments. On a beautiful sunny day, while taking a long walk with one of my best friends, I received a call from the radiation oncologist. He informed me about a new radiation treatment protocol for my type of diagnosis. It wasn't new in the medical world, but new to Manitoba. It called for only five days of radiotherapy. That's it! He went on to cite many studies where it had been proven to be as effective as the sessions that lasted for weeks. When he asked me if I was interested in trying it I squealed, "Sold!" If someone had told me a few months earlier that I'd one day be excited over the prospect of having five radiation treatments to my breast, I would've thought they were out of their mind. My "set up' appointment was about two weeks before the radiation treatments were scheduled to begin. They marked the side of my rib cage with tattoos. A little black dot on either side so they could line me up perfectly with the machine. The only tattoos on my skin, and they're not even pretty!

A word about the staff at Cancer Care Manitoba. They are all low-flying angels. Just to make sure, I looked at their back's when they turned around and sure enough, I swear I could see the outline of wings. They were kind, caring, gentle, respectful and sensitive. During every radiation treatment, I meditated and envisioned that every cell in my body became phosphorescent with a most beautiful light shield to protect my healthy tissues. The only dark spot was where the tumor had been, and that's the only place the radiation was allowed to go. It was such a powerful image of protection. I truly felt, and still feel to this day, that my healthy tissues have been unharmed.

The only thing you can wear into the scanner room is your footwear, and a shapeless off-the-rack gown in a color that'd be unflattering on ANY complexion. I didn't look or feel stunning in a blue hospital gown, so for my five days of radiation I decided to put my own signature on my outfits. For the first four days, I wore a different pair of wild Fluevogs and stunning lipstick. On my final day, I wore a pair of Doc Marten work boots with a four-inch platform heel so I could kick cancer's ass! My footwear became a source of conversation among the nurses, and there were plenty of laughs and giggles every morning. Their job was hard, seeing sick or dying people every day, and I wasn't one of those people! I wanted to help start their days with laughter, health, joy, and happiness and that's what we did together! On the day of my final treatment, they came in to tell me the session was complete, and it was time to get up. I smiled and said, "No, you guys go ahead. I'm in my happy place. I'll just stay here for a bit." We laughed and shared a quiet moment of celebration together for my last day there.

That period of my life was filled with extraordinary stress, significant health issues, loss of work and income, social isolation, and a plethora of other things I won't go into, but it was also the perfect opportunity to put into practice everything I'd been teaching for years as an Occupational Therapist and international speaker on health and wellbeing. I put it all to the test, and you know what? All of it works!

I'm going to give you a quick rundown of everything I did during that time.

I've spent decades of my life eating healthy food. Food can create metabolic stressors in the body, so I've done extensive research. A few years ago, I was privileged to encounter the work of Canadian author, television show host, and holistic nutritionist, Julie Daniluk. Her anti-inflammatory lifestyle is arguably the most seamless blend of western science and research combined with eastern, Ayurvedic, and traditional Chinese medicine practices. Discovering her work and embarking upon her twenty-one-day detoxification program (one of the most beautiful elimination programs you can imagine) changed my life. I even met her and her husband while on a business trip in Toronto and filmed a testimonial because of my profound results. After being diagnosed with cancer, I consulted with Julie to determine the best protocol for my diet. I had already given up sugar, but it was indicated by numerous studies that I needed a low-carb ketogenic diet. My naturopath, who specializes in cancer, endorsed the same type of eating plan. Additionally, Julie recommended a tracking app which I found to be extremely valuable.

One thing you'll notice when going through something devastating is that what you're willing to accept becomes smaller and smaller. At first, when I was prepping for the biopsy, I thought to myself, "I can go through this, it's probably just a cyst or a fatty deposit. A little bit of trauma and everything will be fine." Then you find out it's way more, and you think "Okay, I'm willing to accept that this needs to be removed. It's probably benign and that'll be the end of it." Then the biopsy results come back and it's not good. Then you tell yourself, "If I don't have to go through radiation, chemotherapy or lose my breast, I'll be fine. I can accept that." Then you meet with the surgeon and they ask if you've decided between having a mastectomy or a lumpectomy. "Okay, wasn't expecting that, but I'll accept a lumpectomy." Surely that must be it, but no. Then you hear that there'll be radiation and possible chemo treatments. At that point, you're like, "Oh my gosh. Please let it just be radiation. Please!" That's how fast your world can shrink. You begin by being willing to accept certain things, and your forced to narrow down your focus like a laser beam.

But there's a powerful truth and lesson here. If you can find gratitude in the face of devastation, you're bulletproof. I did exactly that, and discovered gratitude is the greatest gift! I'd used gratitude exercises in the past, but it became part of a daily ritual that was non-negotiable. I had to up my gratitude game. My daily practice was to find twenty things that I was grateful to have experienced in the past 24 hours. The second part was offering thanks for my health, and the health of those I love. The last part was choosing three words that described what I wanted to experience or who I wished to become. Sometimes, I'd choose words like calm, peaceful, and hopeful. Other times, I'd choose words like fearless, strong, and vibrant. The words I chose became a guide for how my days would unfold. I was intentionally creating my experiences and it was life-changing!

During that time, I continued my appointments with my body talk therapist. I was determined to continue the work of unearthing the issues in my tissues. I wanted to keep my Chi flowing unrestricted!

Another daily ritual was meditation. There are so many ways to do this, and I strongly encourage you to find a way to incorporate daily meditation into your life. Please stop telling yourself you don't have time, your kids distract you, or any other thing you say to convince yourself you can't do it. If you're content and happy with every single aspect of your life, then maybe you don't need it. Otherwise, it's a game-changer when it comes to your health and well-being. I had many beautiful and special experiences in meditation. I received edifying words like divine, loving, precious, deserving, and cherished. Words that confirmed to me I was being cared for and watched over. I experienced deep and sustained peace. I even had visits from my deceased mother while deep in mediation. Several inexplicable things happened that strengthened my heart as I navigated my way through uncertain waters.

Exercise was also part of my daily routine, but not in the same way I'd done it in the past. I switched my favored heavy weight and high intensity interval training for walking outside, Pilates, block therapy, and Qi Gong. Those were the things my mindbody craved. I listened and did what felt right. I became my body's ally instead of a taskmaster. No more pushing, shoving, or shaming! It was time I showed myself love.

Speaking of love, something I invested a lot of time and energy in during that time was self-love. I tried to show myself, even in the smallest ways, that I was important and loved. My mother used to say, "You eat with your eyes first," so every meal I consumed was visually appealing, perfectly delicious, healthy, and made with love. I purposed every day to do or experience something that filled my heart. I avoided people who didn't feel like "my people." Anyone prone to negativity or playing the role of perpetual victim weren't allowed in my close circle. In short, I avoided people who increased my levels of stress. I even stopped listening to the news or watching anything that was distressing.

One of the greatest acts of self-care for a nurturer is to learn to receive. This was clearly a stumbling block for me and was tied into powerlessness, perfectionism, and my need to please. Basically, I sucked at it! I was the giver, not a receiver. In order to untangle the false story, I'd brought with me from childhood, I had to accept and KNOW I was worthy of receiving. The Universe obliged and delivered that lesson many times in those intense days of healing. I'm happy to report that I'm now a recovering full-time giver who's able to both give AND receive!

One of the best self-care strategies I implemented was learning to ask for help; to talk about what was difficult, what I needed, and to share with my people. I am beyond blessed with my tribe and having them in my life is a privilege and honor! My tribe is my family of blood, plus my family of choice. Each one of them is like a soul brother or soul sister. They have been brought by special delivery into my life and were with me every step of the way. I learned to be honest, and to receive their love and kindness. It's true that joy shared is joy doubled, and sorrow shared is sorrow halved. I was focused on only experiencing things that filled my heart with joy, peace, and contentment. For the first time in my life, I was ready to tackle any conflict that came up. I would not allow anger or negative emotions to sit inside me and become issues in my tissues. I stepped into my power and dealt with everything that came up, whenever it came up. No passive aggressive BS, and no burying my head in the sand. I learned to pull my big girl panties up and take care of myself. It wasn't easy at the time, but the payoff was huge!

Laughter was another daily part of my stress prevention plan. There were days where my funny bone seemed to be dislocated, but I always managed to find someone who could make me laugh. What a gift to be able to bring laughter to another human, especially one who is suffering! I shamelessly sought out the laughter brokers, those in my tribe who were certain to get me smiling, if not straight up chuckling. My son and daughter were frequent "dealers" for my much-needed giggle fix. I opted for comedies when I decided to watch Netflix in the evenings. I needed the medicine that only laughter could bring and falling asleep while remembering the laughs of the day was just blissful!

Changing your thinking is much harder than changing your actions, and this was one area I was going to have to spend a lot of time working on. When you're dealing with a potentially life-threatening disease or traumatic event, fear is 100% natural. However, you already know how harmful it can be. Given my diagnosis, I had extra motivation to deal with fear so it wouldn't increase my risk of becoming sick. I wasn't sick, and I didn't want to be. I had simply received a diagnosis. Overcoming fear meant challenging my thoughts, and I did that on a daily basis. Slowly but surely, I took control of the fear by asking myself questions like, "Is that really true? Do you know that for sure?" Or I would make statements like, "Just because that's a common side effect doesn't mean YOU will have it." By the way, I'm well known for saying "I don't do side effects!" And guess what—I don't! Basically, I was taking my brain to the mental gym and training it to no longer live in fear. It took persistence and a lot of work to pull myself out of that habitual way of thinking, but can you think of anything more worthwhile than transforming your negative, symptom-producing thought patterns to ones that are life-giving? It was epic! I found an inner strength I had never experienced. I was never prone to being negative, but I was definitely prone to fear and anxiety. They no longer hold me hostage. I've learned that by challenging myself, I can move in a different direction. My health and happiness bear witness to that change. When you stop living in denial, you can move into survival. From there, thriving is a quick step forward.

My antidote to fear was trust, coupled with two deeply held convictions. First, everything happens for a reason. Second, I had a proven track record that I could get through anything. WE ALL DO! Every tough, traumatic, or difficult thing you've faced is in the past. Whatever you're facing in the present will soon be in the past as well. I surrendered to these truths and the peacefulness that came with it is difficult to describe.

Fear wasn't the only thing I had to tackle. There was also anger. That said, when I confronted my anger, I found it was grounded in fear. Sometimes, what you feel on the surface isn't the whole story. You have to dig deep and uncover what's hidden beneath. My anger was rooted in my fear that nothing I was doing would make a difference in my overall health. After all, I had done everything right and still ended up being diagnosed with cancer, so could I even trust myself to create health? I discussed the evidence with myself, recognizing that the more I could control the better my chances. I reminded myself of the evidence I already possessed. The amazing outcomes regarding my surgeries, healing, treatment options, and more. The investment I'd made in my health, up until that point, allowed me to sail through all of that in an incredible way. My life was full of ordinary miracles! I made a commitment to do my very best for myself and for the sake of my children. I would give myself the best possibility for optimum health. This meant an ongoing, super-sized, non-negotiable investment in my physical, emotional, mental, and spiritual well-being. So many people stop when they feel better. Once you've lost the weight, the exercise and eating plan falls off. Once you've recovered from injury, you stop doing the stretches recommended by your physical therapist. You know what I'm talking about, it happens all the time. I was determined to not let that happen. I was given a second chance, and there was no way I was going to blow it. I would put my well-being above everything, every day, because I was the only one who could!

When the pandemic came along and upended our entire world, there were so many things going on in my life at the time. Diagnosis, surgeries, radiation, infections, loss of work, income, and social connection—and that's not even a complete list! There were other personal issues I've not spoken about publicly. It was a horrific time, and not just for me, but for millions of others around the world.

If there's one thing I learned from being diagnosed with cancer, it's the power of intention. The opposite of that is letting your day happen by accident, fate, or chance. I refused to be a victim of chance or fate, so I began my own intention therapy on full display via social media. I began creating posts called *I'm Testing "Positive."* Every day I posted something that began with a phrase something like, "I'm testing 'positive' today, care to join me?" In truth, these posts were for my own personal therapy, but I thought what helped me might also help others, so I put them all on every social media platform I was using. Each day I set an intention to create something positive in my day, a focus, a guiding light to help me move forward in my healing. It didn't just work for me, it resonated with my followers and online connections. People even began reposting! It was a beautiful ripple effect or butterfly effect in action! That beautiful, daily practice expanded into the inspiration to create this book.

That brings to mind another beautiful concept regarding a deeper understanding of stress and health. What you focus on expands! Surely, you've experienced this. You have a day that starts off bad, and it just goes downhill from there. You fixate on how crappy your morning was, and before you know it you're attracting every mishap or Murphy's Law situation imaginable. Other times it's the opposite. Your day starts off great and it just gets better as the day goes on. All because you were focused on the good stuff. What you focus on grows and attracts more of the same. When I was going through the health challenges I described earlier, the only thing I wanted to focus on was health and vitality. When opposite feelings arose, I doubled up on the self-love and pictured in my mind everything I wanted to do when I felt more energized. It worked! What I'm telling you isn't a theory, because I put it to the ultimate test and it worked for me. Every single time!

Another thing that enhanced my ability to go through the challenges I faced with resilience and improved health was something I avoided. Not once did I ever say, "I have cancer." I may have said I was diagnosed with it, but never that I "had" it. It didn't become my identity and I certainly didn't own it. I went so far with that mindset that I wouldn't even read anything about my diagnosis, nor any material the doctor's office sent home with me. I listened with one ear to descriptions of side effects, statistics on reoccurrence, symptoms, and future outcomes.

I'm not advising others to take that approach; I'm simply sharing what I chose to do for myself. In my own head and heart I knew, "I don't do side effects. I don't do probabilities. I don't do re-occurrences. I don't do cancer." You become what you believe, and I wanted to believe in my ability to create health.

My heart breaks when I hear people define themselves with labels. I remember working with an injured worker who told me, "The doctor says my knee is bone on bone and I'll probably be in a wheelchair before long." I just looked at him and said, "And you accept that?! You're to going say 'Oh well, I guess that's the way it's going to be?' Surely you're not going to accept this without a fight. Let's get to work on getting your knee stronger, and let's prove your doctor wrong! He doesn't know you, or your determination and attitude. Let's do this together!" We went to work and I'm happy to report he didn't end up in a wheelchair.

The bottom line is you create your own reality. Guard your tongue, not just in relation to others, but in relation to yourself. Be loving and kind, and do not hang labels on yourself! You will become what you label yourself to be. When you tell yourself you're stupid or weak, that you're unable to do or be something, you will be right. But here's the catch, you can't just say, "Well, I don't do side effects," and then not actually believe that. You have to trust AND believe what you say to and about yourself. I learned and lived these things firsthand.

Maybe you know the right words to say to yourself, but are wondering, "How do I get to the believing part?" What I did was use evidence or questions. For example: When the doctors informed me about the probability the cancer would reoccur I asked myself, "If the probability is 10 percent of it returning, isn't the probability of no recurrence 90 percent? Why can't you be in that category? What would get you into that category?" Other times I used past evidence to help me believe. I could think of many times in my life when a positive attitude made all the difference. I remembered all the times I challenged my fears and had a positive outcome. I didn't need to look far to know that I could truly believe what I was saying to and about myself.

Dear readers, it would be a huge understatement to say I'm humbled that you're reading this book and are open to sharing this experience with me. I'm keenly aware that my purpose on Earth is to create hope, ease suffering, and teach people to create their own health and well-being. Thank you for giving me the opportunity to do so in your life. Please know and believe in your infinite power to create change in your life. Never give that gift to someone else. If you expect others to somehow make you happy or healthy, you will be disappointed. That privilege and responsibility is yours alone.

To get the most out of this book, choose a page to read at the beginning of each day, and answer the self-reflection questions. The precious few moments you spend doing that will shape all the moments that follow. I hope you'll create the life you want on purpose as you stop allowing the days, weeks, months, and years, to unfold by accident or default. Be intentional with every day, time is not unlimited. Put out what you hope will come back to you. Not only because you want it back, but because it's the right thing to do. For all the love you give to others, I'm wishing for you to receive ten times that amount in return. I'm wishing you health, happiness, success, and incredible abundance! I'm wishing you many days that fill your heart and soul with awe!

It's true that your life is in your own hands, and only you can determine its direction, but that doesn't mean you walk alone. We need each other. Regardless of experience or level of education, no one person has all the answers. Everyone stumbles sometimes, and during those times we can lean on one another. This is how we learn and grow. As humans, we're hard-wired to thrive within a supportive community. We may not be able to heal each other, but we can help each other heal. Whatever we may be capable of as individuals, we can do more together. I'm here for you, just as I know you'd be there for me. Together, we will rise. Remember this beautiful quote from Ram Dass, "We're all just walking each other home."

Thank you for walking with me on this journey.

"A positive attitude causes a chain
reaction of positive thoughts,
events, and outcomes.
It is a catalyst and it sparks
extraordinary results."

- Unknown

Day 1

W ho doesn't love to be around someone with a positive attitude? Their energy just feels good and is magnetic. Emotions like love, joy, happiness, and gratitude, are high frequency emotions that attract experiences that amplify those feelings.

The opposite is also true.

The lower frequency emotions like anger, shame, doubt, and fear also attract like-frequency experiences.

If you want your life to change, start with changing your internal emotional state.

What emotional state characterizes your typical day?

_____

_____

Shifting your focus helps. What can you shift your focus to in order to change your internal emotional state?

_____

_____

"A steadfast heart does not stray from the path."

- Wayne Gerard Trotman

Day 2

Here's a great way to test positive today. When life is in a state of flux or chaos, thinking about what is constant, or steadfast, in your life can really help you stay grounded.

Focusing on things like your family, friendships, health practices, hobbies, meaningful work, and positive emotions, can change your vibrational energy and help you stay calm during chaos.

What are the constants in your life that add value?

_____

_____

How did focusing on these things change your perspective today?

_____

_____

"I enjoy spreading positivity because spreading negativity is too much work."

- Unknown

Day 3

A sense of accomplishment is a great way to test positive. Accomplishing something causes a beautiful cascade of "feel good" hormones that make you feel happier, more content, and less stressed.

Get outside and do some yardwork, and get the added benefit of vitamin D, or tackle some indoor jobs that don't get done daily like vacuuming under furniture, extra cleaning, bathrooms, and dusting under knickknacks. When you have the feeling of accomplishing something, you can't help but feel positive, which will spread to everyone around you.

What tasks did you accomplish?

_____

_____

How does it feel to be done?

_____

_____

Positive Mind,

Positive Vibes,

Positive Life.

Day 4

A couple of days ago, we talked about grounding yourself by remembering the things in your life that are constant. Today, testing positive is about change. Changing things up can create a big wave of healthy hormones that will leave you happier and more content—so get out of your routine today!

Try walking a different route than you normally do, or try adding a unique food item to your menu. Go shopping at a different store, or read an article on a subject you wouldn't normally read. A fresh perspective can change everything.

What did you do to change it up today?

_____

_____

In what way did that change your feelings about the day?

_____

_____

"Mindfulness is the aware,
balanced acceptance of
the present experience."

- Sylvia Boorstein

Day 5

Mindfulness is a wonderful way to test positive. and there are many ways you can experience more of it in your life. Today, try a mindfulness meditation while you are taking a walk outside. You'll get the added benefit of vitamin D, which is crucial to a healthy immune system.

Here's how this works:

As you walk, focus on the five senses. What do you see, hear, feel, smell, and taste while you're walking. This meditation helps you stay focussed on the present moment, calms your nervous system, and helps you produce more serotonin and endorphins—so good for your physical and emotional well-being!

How did this brief meditation work for you, were you able to stay focused on the senses?

_____

_____

What did you notice on your walk that you've never paid attention to before?

_____

_____

"Sometimes, all it takes to change your life is to change your routine."

- Stephen Richards

Day 6

A great way to test positive during the change of seasons (if you have seasons) is to mark the transition with a change in your routine.

During these transition times, accelerate your excitement for the change by packing up clothing of the current season, and taking out the clothing for the upcoming season. Put on some music that's appropriate for the approaching season, such as Christmas music or something that feels like spring, while you prepare to begin your garden by ordering seeds, plants, and so on.

Having something to look forward to produces positive hormones which make you feel great.

What did you do today to mark the upcoming change of season?

_____

_____

How can you feel more hopeful and prepared?

_____

_____

"I am a person who
works well under pressure.
In fact, I work so well under
pressure that at times, I will
procrastinate in order to create
this pressure."

- Stephanie Pearl-McPhee

Day 7

Procrastination is a quick way to kill joy and add more stress to your life. You'll definitely not be testing positive if you're putting off things that need to be done.

Procrastination is self-destructive, but accomplishment creates a flood of positive neurochemicals that pour into your system and decreases the feeling of stress. Today is a great day to work on tasks that you have been putting off.

What are the top three tasks that have been nagging at you? Can you start tackling them today?

_____

_____

What is the barrier to getting things done? In other words what's keeping you stuck in procrastination and experiencing its negative affects?

_____

_____

"No act of kindness, no matter how small, is ever wasted."

- Aesop

Day 8

A great way to get yourself out of a negative state of mind, and into a positive one, is to look for opportunities to help someone else.

It could be something as simple as opening a door, checking in on a friend, or returning someone's grocery cart. Your body produces more serotonin when you perform an act of kindness for someone else. It's also a great way to get out of your head and into your heart.

What did you do today for someone else?

_____

_____

How did your act kindness make you feel? What effect do you think it had on the recipient?

_____

_____

"Never underestimate the power of a planted seed."

- Unknown

Day 9

C hallenging times come to all of us at some point. I gave an online presentation a while back where I shared a simple analogy I believe will help you test positive today, even if things are difficult right now.

In order for a seed to grow into its potential, something needs to crack the seed's covering. In other words, it needs to be broken in order for it to become a beautiful plant. A seed's drive to survive, in spite of adversity, is then passed to the plant, where it will strive to grow in even the most hostile environment. Think of the way the roots of a tree will push through the cement of a sidewalk.

Today, focus on what you'll see in three months time, in your own growth and development. What fruit and possibilities will come from the difficult time you've experienced? Something amazing is germinating right now!

What do you think could be the possible growth, silver lining, or good that might come from this difficult time?

_____

_____

How can the possibility of growth keep you going through this difficulty instead of staying stuck in it?

_____

_____

"Don't let the fear of what could happen make nothing happen."

- Doe Zantamata

Day 10

A huge obstacle to testing positive is fear. My favorite way to define fear is: **F**alse **E**vidence **A**ppearing **R**eal. Much of what we fear is created in our mind, but not evidenced in reality. Think of how you feel when your boss asks to see you in their office. Even if you have a good relationship with your boss, you still feel a little bit of fear-based stress because of the potential scenarios you've created in your mind. Today's a great day to focus on what you know for sure.

Ask yourself, "What do I know for sure?"

Often the answers to these questions will help settle your nervous system and get you out of the stress and fear response. Meditation can also help refocus your mind on the power you have to control your thoughts and emotions.

What's scaring you today?

_____

_____

What strategy did you use to confront the fear? How did that work?

_____

_____

"If you change the way you look at things, the things you look at change."

- Wayne Dyer

Day 11

Have you noticed that you default to a negative perspective on life? How often do you complain about the weather? Or a coworker? It's almost automatic isn't it? Testing positive takes effort and intention. In other words, you have to do it on purpose.

Today is a great day to focus on a more positive perspective, one that leaves you happy, peaceful, healthy, and content. It starts with the words you use. Change your words, change your world!

If you caught yourself having negative thoughts today, how were you able to switch them to something more positive?

_____

_____

What makes it difficult for you to adopt a positive perspective?

_____

_____

"Life begins at the end of
your comfort zone."

- Neal Donald Walsch

Day 12

What comes to mind when you hear the phrase "comfort zone?" Does it make you feel anxious or excited? Intentionally focusing on the positive means allowing yourself to be outside your comfort zone with excitement instead of anxiety. This is completely within your control. In fact, it's your choice. Anxiety can cause physiological harm by producing stress hormones. However, feelings of excitement and anticipation will do the opposite.

It's important to give yourself the opportunity to experience being outside of your comfort zone by intentionally choosing a positive emotional perspective. Plus, it'll help build resilience and train you to manage stress in a different way.

What experience did you give yourself today that was outside of your comfort zone?

_____

_____

What was the outcome, and how did it affect the way you feel?

_____

_____

"Daring to set boundaries is about having the courage to love ourselves even when we risk disappointing others."

- Brené Brown

Day 13

R adical self-care is a great way to test positive! One of the most important self-care practices I've learned is setting boundaries. You teach people how you want to be treated. If you allow people to be disrespectful, unkind, or rude, it teaches them that you're okay with it.

Setting boundaries is an effective way of letting people know what you expect, and what you will or will not tolerate. Think of it like this: What you permit, you promote.

You may need to create boundaries with yourself too. A little self-control goes a long way toward keeping stress under control.

Which relationship, or relationships, in your life needs some new boundaries?

_____

_____

Think of someone (including yourself) with whom you need to set boundaries, and then do it. How does it feel?

_____

_____

"Anticipation of pleasure
is a pleasure in itself."

- Sylvia Townsend Warner

Day 14

Do you know what creates instant positivity? Anticipation! Today's a great day to plan something cool, amazing, fun, and indulgent.

Anticipation is so magical, not just for the river of positive, stress-busting, health-enhancing hormones it releases into your body, but also because it's a two-for-one mental health strategy. You get the "feel good" benefits in the present moment, and you'll experience them again when you're enjoying what you've planned. Joy today, and joy tomorrow!

What can you plan to do that will create anticipation now, and joy when you're able to see your plan come together?

_____

_____

What can you plan with others, but also something just for you?

_____

_____

"As I say yes to life,
life says yes to me!"

- Louise Hay

Day 15

As you get older, have you noticed you're less in touch with your intuition and gut feelings? A sure way to test positive is to start tuning into yourself again. One way to do that is to find ways to say "yes" to opportunities, instead of immediately saying "no."

When an opportunity comes your way, fear often makes you react with a "no" without even considering whether it's possible or not. Do not confuse fear with intuition, sometimes they work together, but often they do not. Fear is usually tied to the unknown. If you feel compelled to reject an opportunity because it's unfamiliar, that's probably fear talking.

Today's a great day to find a way to say "yes" to something that could be an amazing opportunity for you.

What were you able to say "yes" to today that you might've previously rejected?

_____

_____

What opportunities have you passed on in the past because fear made you say no?

_____

_____

"Sometimes life takes you into a dark place where you feel it's impossible to breathe. You think you've been buried, but don't give up, because if truth be told, you've actually been planted."

- Karen Gibbs

Day 16

D o you ever wake up with fear, anxiety, or dark thoughts? Thankfully, it doesn't happen to me very often, but it does happen. When mornings come with dark thoughts, I have strategies that help me test positive in spite of them.

If this is you today, try shifting things with a little help from your friends! Reach out to a friend who always puts a smile on your face, or helps ease the burden of negative emotions. Cuddle with your pets to produce oxytocin, the cuddling hormone which helps you break free of the stress response brought on by dark thoughts. Or engage in a small act of self-care, like coffee in bed or eating some dark chocolate.

Remember, the sun always shines after the rain. Even the darkest night is followed by a sunrise.

What strategy did you use to break free from dark thoughts or emotions today?

_____

_____

How effective was that strategy? And if it wasn't, what could you try next time?

_____

_____

"The only person who can
stop you from reaching
your goals is you."

- Jackie Joyner-Kersee

Day 17

W hen you're diligently working on your health goals, it's difficult when the people living with you aren't on the same path. It's a challenge to stay the course without support and encouragement. But do you really need anyone else's permission or help? Nope!

Don't compromise your choices or your goals! If you choose to exercise daily, don't let the enticement of sitting on the couch with your family stop you from getting your workout done. Work out while you watch! If everyone wants pizza for dinner, and that's not on your healthy menu, create a substitution that works for you. You're the only person who can help you reach goals, and the only person who can prevent you from reaching goals is you.

What health goal were you able to stick to today in spite of a lack of support, or even some nudging to drop your goal for the day?

_____

_____

What strategy can you use to stop yourself from compromising or stepping away from your goals in the future?

_____

_____

"The most important three words you can say to yourself: Yes I can!"

- Denis Waitley

Day 18

Testing positive takes intention and effort. So often, we limit ourselves with our own self talk. We might say things like "There's nothing I can do" or "I can't."

Today is a great day to look at some of the unsolvable issues that have come up over the last few weeks and instead of saying "I can't", ask yourself "How can I?" The first statement makes you a victim, whereas the question presumes victory.

It's been said that, "Whether you think you can, or think you can't, you're right."

What situation have you faced that seemed unsolvable? How did you tackle it with a "How can I?" attitude?

_____

_____

How did shifting perspective affect your feelings about a problem that seemed unsolvable?

_____

_____

"It's not selfish to love yourself,
take care of yourself, and to
make your happiness a priority.
It's necessary."

- Mandy Hale

Day 19

Radical self-care is a beautiful way to test positive! People who are nurturers tend to put themselves last on their own to-do list. It's easy to get so busy looking after everyone else that you forget to look after yourself—until you start to break down. Today's a great day to take some time and look after you! One way I like to do this is taking care of my skin with a special beauty treatment. I choose to use all natural products as much as possible. Here is a great one for dry skin that you can make yourself:

- One cup of grapeseed oil.
- 2/3 of a cup of sea salt.
- 16 drops of essential oil. I like to use lavender and eucalyptus.

Combine the ingredients and mix thoroughly. Rub the mixture on dry skin, shower off and pat your skin dry. You can use this over your entire body and face.

What self-care ritual makes you feel rejuvenated? Treat yourself!

_____

_____

How did you choose to care for yourself today? How did it change the way you felt?

_____

_____

"There is no such thing as
a small act of kindness.
Every act creates a ripple
with no logical end."

- Scott Adams

Day 20

Today's a great day to test positive by doing something for someone who is struggling. There are always people in your life who would benefit from a phone call, text message, visit, or a small gift that says "I care."

The cool thing about performing acts of kindness is that your body will release the "happy hormones" serotonin and dopamine. These feel-good chemicals will improve your mood and soothe anxiety, which is healthy for your body too. Even more incredible is that the person on the receiving end of acts of kindness enjoys the same benefits. It's a beautiful energetic boomerang!

What small acts of kindness can you share with someone in your circle who is struggling today?

_____

_____

What small acts of kindness can you offer to YOURSELF today?

_____

_____

"When you replace
'Why is this happening to me'?
with
'What is this trying to teach me?'

Everything shifts."

- Unknown

Day 21

Have you asked yourself, "Why me?" It isn't easy to test positive when you feel like nothing is going your way, but this question is completely disempowering. It leaves you feeling like a victim of fate, the gods, the wind, the universe, or whatever you believe in. It's impossible to have hope when you feel like a victim.

Today is a great day to ask "Why NOT me?" You have what it takes to get through every difficult circumstance in life. In fact, you've already done this because you've made it through 100% of all the tough days you've had in the past. If you feel stuck, take your power back by making a change, stepping forward and away from feeling like a victim.

What good could possibly come out of a difficult situation that you might face today?

_____

_____

What step can you take in order to move forward?

_____

_____

"You can complain about the direction of your life all you want, but until you sit in the driver's seat and begin to drive yourself, you aren't going to get where you want to go!"

- Les Brown

Day 22

A re you a complainer? Did you know that complaining causes increased inflammation in your body and activates stress hormones that will harm your health if you do so consistently? Today's a great day to test positive by not uttering a single complaint about anything.

Focus on enhancing your physical and mental well-being with only positive statements, and experience the positive effect it has on your day!

How difficult was it to avoid complaining?

_____

_____

What did you notice about your day, or your interactions, by being more positive?

_____

_____

"A good laugh heals a lot
of hurts."

- Madeline L'Engle

Day 23

Today's a great day to be more positive by bringing a little laughter into your day.

They say laughter is the best medicine, and that's true. Laughter causes your body to produce endorphins, and research shows that even witnessing laughter can bring about the same physiological reaction. It's great to be able to laugh at yourself, but other times you may need to reach out to that certain friend or family member who makes you laugh. Every. Single. Time.

Or maybe there's a great comedy series or movie that'll have you giggling in no time. Whatever you have to do, find some reasons to laugh today.

What made you laugh (even if it's just on the inside) today?

_____

_____

How do you bring the gift of laughter to the people you love?

_____

_____

"Forgive yourself for not
having the foresight to
know what now seems so
obvious in hindsight"

- Judy Belmont

Day 24

Hindsight is 20/20. There's little doubt you've heard, and likely spoken, that expression many times. Have you ever had a terrible experience, but when you look back on it you realize everything worked out for the best? That's the value of hindsight. What if you could use hindsight in the present moment? For example, what if you could look at a circumstance that is difficult right now and ask yourself, "When I look back on this in three months, what good will I say came out of it?

Keep your focus on the possibility that there could be some good (or maybe even amazing) things that'll come from what you're experiencing today. It'll shift your perspective, enhance your sense of well-being, and help you test positive!

What are some good things that may come from this difficult time that you are going through?

_____

_____

Think of a difficult time that you went through in the past, what good things came from it?

_____

_____

"You were born with the ability to change someone's life, don't ever waste it."

- Dale Partridge

Day 25

I t's true that we have to be reminded to take care of ourselves, but sometimes the best action to take when you're struggling emotionally is to make it all about someone else. Researchers have called it a "helpers high," because you get back what you give out. It's another energetic boomerang, just like the acts of kindness thing we talked about earlier this month. If you're feeling a little low today, it might be a great time to make it all about someone else. Maybe a coworker or family member would really enjoy a surprise dinner invite, game or some other fun experience. It might just be exactly what you need.

Several years ago, I was left in charge at my job while my boss was away. I had to hold a team meeting and decided to start off with a ridiculous and fun game. No one expected it. I could've made it all about me because I was in charge. Instead, I made sure everyone had fun, and that was the most enjoyable meeting we had that year!

What did you do to make it all about someone else today?

_____

_____

How did bringing some fun to others change YOUR day?

_____

_____

"The invariable mark
of wisdom is to see the
miraculous in the common."

- Ralph Waldo Emerson

Day 26

Sometimes, the things we think are small and inconsequential are the very things that make the biggest difference. I love being in nature and tuning in to the joy of walking. No fanfare, large crowds, or talking—just walking. Going to the gym is fun, but our primitive brains are most at home in nature. It's a place where we experience a true connection to life. Nature offers us so many beautiful lessons, if we'll only take the time to listen and observe. It's a seemingly small thing, but it makes a huge difference.

Today's a great day to get outside and experience the miracle of being alive. Go for a walk in nature. Everything around you is bursting with energy and life. Isn't it amazing how the beautiful, big trees were once tiny little seeds filled with unlimited potential?

The same is true for you and me. Our potential is unlimited!

How can you get some time outside today so you can experience the peace nature provides?

_____

_____

What effect did it have on the negative emotions that you may have been experiencing?

_____

_____

"Dance like nobody is watching, because they're not, they're all checking their phones!"

- Unknown

Day 27

It's hard to be negative when you're doing something fun and silly. Children shouldn't have the monopoly on fun! Today's a great day to do something silly.

Dance like no one is watching, because no one is watching! Wear a silly hat when you leave the house and enjoy the smiles you create. Do a magic trick for a child in the grocery store. Video yourself and friends doing something fun and post it online.

You're only limited by your imagination!

What silliness or fun did you instigate today?

_____

_____

What effect did it have on you and others?

_____

_____

"Don't listen to what people say, look at what they do. Actions speak louder than words."

- Unknown

Day 28

Y ou've heard the expression "Actions speak louder than words." Words are easy to say, but if there's no action to back them up, they lose their power. We're taught when we're young to say things like, "I'm sorry" or "Thank you" and often we utter those words automatically with little thought. For example, you bump into someone at the store and you mutter, "Oh, sorry." But are you really?

When my children were very young, I taught them to pair actions with their words. Show through your behavior that you mean what you say. It makes all the difference.

Can you show someone how you really feel, and not just say the words? How will you do it?

_____

_____

Are you aware of your own love language, and can you recognize the love language of others in your life?

_____

_____

"Thinking will not overcome
fear but action will."

- W. Clement Stone

Day 29

It can be tough to test positive when you're scared. Do you ever wake up with fear in your belly because of something you have to do later in the day? Instead of letting fear take over your day and ruin your health, you can own it with effort and intention.

See yourself owning that fear and having power over it. Visualize it in your mind. If it's a difficult conversation with someone who's intimidating, you might imagine yourself as the more confident and calm individual. You can even picture yourself as being physically taller. You can use a similar mindset to face any tough situation. When I was battling cancer, and had go in for my first day of radiation treatment, I strutted into the building wearing a stunning pair of four-inch Doc Martens—ready to kick me some radiation a$$!

What were you afraid of today, and was that fear realistic?

_____

_____

What other strategies can you use to see yourself bigger than your fear and reclaim your power?

_____

_____

"No matter how I feel, I get up, dress up, and show up for life. When I do, the day always serves up more than I could have hoped for. Each day truly is a slice of heaven. Some days the slices are just smaller than others."

- Regina Brett

Day 30

Testing positive isn't about swallowing negative emotions. It's about recognizing that, with intention and effort, even difficult times can have positive outcomes. Sometimes, you have to change your feelings before you feel like changing your actions. You're not going to feel like hugging someone if you're angry, so the anger needs to change before you can hug them.

Other times, if you change your actions, your feelings will follow. For example, if you wake up grumpy, but go to work with a smile on your face, eventually that smile becomes genuine. Some may call this a "fake it till you make it" technique, but in Sylvia-speak it's more like, "chin up, shoulders back, grab some sass and take on the day!"

What's easier for you to change, feelings or actions? What does it depend on?

_____

_____

Did you try the "fake it till you make it" (or Sylvia-speak) strategy today? How did your feelings change as a result?

_____

_____

"Surrender and accept that whatever is happening in the moment, the Universe is working on your behalf."

- Mastin Kipp

Day 31

Where are all my control freaks at?! You got to admit, we all have control issues sometimes. Sometimes, testing positive involves surrender. Surrendering is not giving up. In fact, it's a position of power because you're acknowledging that everything is exactly as it is, and is intended for your benefit and growth.

We typically become so focused on creating change, that we forget there are times when letting go of control is the way out.

Let go and watch what happens!

What do you need to surrender to, or let go of?

_____

_____

How could letting go of this issue help you?

_____

_____

"Forgive others, not because they deserve forgiveness, but because you deserve peace."

- Jonathan Lockwood Huie

Day 32

It's hard to maintain a positive attitude when you're holding a grudge. They say (whoever "they" are) that being unforgiving is like taking poison and hoping the other person will get sick. But they don't, you do!

Forgiveness is really all about you and your well-being. It's also acknowledging the fact that there are times when you're in need of forgiveness too. And sometimes the person you need to forgive the most is you.

What do you need to focus on forgiving yourself for today?

_____

_____

Are you able to forgive the people in your life who have hurt you? How does this make you feel?

_____

_____

"If you listen to your body
when it whispers, you will never
have to listen to it scream."

- Unknown

Day 33

There are times to push through, and there are times to lean in and listen. Test positive today by leaning in and listening to what your body needs.

Your head and body will argue sometimes. Your head might try to convince you that you're being a slacker or lazy, but your body knows it needs rest. Sometimes, pushing is more harmful than pulling back. Tune in to what you need to do today.

What's your body asking for today?

_____

_____

What can you do today to pause, listen, and give your body what it needs?

_____

_____

"What is something your 9am self can do that your 5pm self will thank you for?"

- Unknown

Day 34

One sure-fire way for testing positive is to plan out your day with the end in mind. Ask yourself how you would like to feel at the end of this day. Proud, satisfied, peaceful? Once you've decided how you want to feel, plan your day in such a way as to guarantee that outcome.

For example, if you want to end the day feeling peaceful, you may choose to not return a call to someone who tends to argue. Or you might decide to make a specific conversational topic off-limits for today. Plan with the end in sight!

How would you like to feel at the end of your day? Choose your feelings and plan accordingly.

_____

_____

How did this strategy work out for you today?

_____

_____

"I learned that courage was not the absence of fear, but the triumph over it. The brave man is not he who does not feel afraid, but he who conquers that fear."

- Nelson Mandela

Day 35

I t's pretty much impossible to test positive when you're afraid. If you're not careful, being fearful can become a habit and you may get addicted to the stress response and the physiological reactions that come with it. Today, choose something you're afraid of and take a step toward conquering your fear. Even a small step can make a big difference. You'll find that fear will often vaporize when you move right into it.

It takes some practice, but developing the habit of conquering fear will strengthen your ability to overcome fears that hold you back.

What fear are you ready to tackle today?

_____

_____

Once you took a step toward fear, was it easier or harder than you thought it would be?

_____

_____

"We rise by lifting others."

- Robert Ingersoll

Day 36

Have you noticed the extremes? Some people are so lovely, while others are seem to be so darn miserable. It's easy to get annoyed by the latter, but those are usually the people who need some extra kindness.

Do you remember what's cool about performing acts of kindness? You benefit as much as the person receiving! The health benefits of being kind are huge, thanks to the resulting biochemical reactions in your body, which includes the production of serotonin, the good mood fluid that leaves you feeling more content.

How did you spread a little extra kindness today?

_____

_____

What effect did it have on you and others?

_____

_____

"The way we spend our time defines who we are."

- Jonathan Estrin

Day 37

What's your love language? One of my favorites is food, and another is giving my time to others. A great way to test positive today is to give your time to someone. It's really not hard to do, and it's a priceless gift.

Time is a finite and precious resource, and when you give some of yours to another it sends a powerful message that says, "I care about you. You're worth it." Do you know someone who needs to hear that message today?

What was your biggest barrier to creating time to gift someone in need today?

_____

_____

How was your gift of time received? Do you feel it was time well spent?

_____

_____

"Be patient.
Good things take time."

- Unknown

Day 38

I t has been said that patience is a virtue. If that's true, then what does that say about impatience? I'd say it's a very unpleasant emotional state to experience! Being impatient creates a lot of unnecessary stress. Today's a great day to understand that things happen for a reason, and sometimes we simply need to wait.

Test positive today by exercising patience. It'll leave you in a more peaceful state of being.

What happened today to test your patience?

_____

_____

Was the day different as a result of your intention to be patient?

_____

_____

"Grace is the face that love wears
when it meets imperfection."

- Joseph R. Cooke

Day 39

I have a dear friend who shared this quote with me, "All things in moderation, except for gratitude and grace." Gratitude is a powerful currency that will change your mood and your health. You can show grace to others, and it doesn't matter if they're deserving or not. That's why it's called grace. It costs you nothing, but it's priceless to those who receive it.

Testing positive today is about focusing on gratitude for everything you have, and showing grace to others.

What are you grateful for today?

_____

_____

Who did you offer grace to and why?

_____

_____

"Set a goal that makes you want to jump out of bed in the morning."

- Unknown

Day 40

Setting and reaching goals is very satisfying. Your chances of success are significantly greater when you outline the steps you'll need to take in order to accomplish your goal. The beauty of having goals is that you get to experience the excitement of setting them, but also a sense of accomplishment with every step you take toward them. Once you've accomplished your goal, you get the amazing experience of celebrating your achievement. I call that a win-win-win situation!

If you're struggling to stay in a positive mindset today, set a small but meaningful goal and take a step towards it. Celebrate the fact you took action, and celebrate again when you've completed the step!

What goal can you set for yourself today? What step (baby steps count) will you take toward it?

_____

_____

How did you feel when you completed the step?

_____

_____

"You always gain
by giving love."

- Reese Witherspoon

Day 41

One of the most beautiful ways you can test positive is to focus on love. Love for self, others, and love for all of the creatures we share our planet with.

When you're in a state of love, you vibrate at a higher frequency, and this beautiful energy changes everyone and everything around you. What you put into the world comes back to you. It's another energetic boomerang!

How can you show or express love to those around you today?

_____

_____

What are some ways you can practice self love today?

_____

_____

"Our intention
creates our reality."

- Wayne Dyer

Day 42

Here's an excellent way to test positive today: Disrupt some of your daily routines. Have you noticed how much of your life is spent on autopilot? Intentional changes create new realities. Let's change it up today!

You could take a different route to work, do something different on your coffee break, listen to new music, or hang out with different people during lunch. Be intentional, and then be amazed.

What routine did you disrupt today?

_____

_____

How did you benefit from changing things up today?

_____

_____

"It is an absolute human certainty that no one can know his own beauty or perceive a sense of his own worth until it has been reflected back to him in the mirror of another loving, caring human being."

- John Joseph Powell

Day 43

A s Ram Dass once said, "We're all just walking each other home." I think that's a beautiful way to think about life. It should be noted that this doesn't always mean you get to choose who's walking beside you, but you can choose how you treat them.

If you see someone stumble, allow them to lean on you. If you see someone fall, lift them up. If you see someone succeeding, cheer them on. It doesn't matter who they are, only that they're a fellow human and you're walking home together. In the end, we all need each other.

Who in your life could use a little support or a helping hand today?

_____

_____

What are some ways you can support or encourage them?

_____

_____

"Stars can't shine
without darkness."

- D.H. Sidebottom

Day 44

Being a light for others is easy when everything's going your way—the light just naturally shines from within you. When you're feeling the opposite, like the darkness is swallowing you up, it doesn't come as easily. However, when you make the choice to shine in spite of circumstances, you not only brighten up the lives of others, but your own as well!

Do you know who sees the light quicker than anyone? The ones in the dark, so grab some shades and shine on!

Who needs your light today?

_____

_____

How can you light up the day for someone who is in darkness?

_____

_____

"The wound is the place
where the Light enters you."

- Rumi

Day 45

Testing positive is not about denying the negative. Not every day is going to be full of sunshine and roses. It's important to allow yourself to fully experience your negative feelings, while still being intentional about moving forward. Being positive simply means you're not focusing all of your attention on negative things or feeding them your energy.

If you want to move forward, you have to hold space for your pain, acknowledge and honor it. Learn what triggers negative feelings, because your triggers are your teachers.

What negative emotions did you acknowledge today?

_____

_____

What can you learn from your triggers?

_____

_____

"I dream my painting
and I paint my dream."

- Vincent van Gogh

Day 46

The law of attraction is real, because energy flows where your attention goes. You'll become what you believe, and the nature of your thoughts will become your reality. In this way, you attract what you think about the most. With these things in mind, what would you like to focus on attracting today?

Creating, visualizing, and taking action toward your goals will help you create an energetic and magnetic pull of attraction. Trust and believe, and you will see for yourself.

What goal would you like to manifest today?

_____

_____

What are your thoughts predominantly focused on, and where are you directing your energy?

_____

_____

"If you only say one prayer in a day make it thank you."

- Rumi

Day 47

Perspective is everything. During difficult times, expressing genuine gratitude will open your eyes to the beautiful things that come from having faced challenging times. Often, those things couldn't come into your life in no other way. Your days are filled with "ordinary" miracles!

Choosing to focus on the good during tough times doesn't mean you're in denial. It means you have faith that the sun is still there, and will shine again after the rain has passed.

Can you think of something you're thankful for today, in spite of any difficulties you may be experiencing?

_____

_____

What are some good things that could come from this tough time?

_____

_____

"I am a master at setting boundaries that protect my time, energy, creativity, and emotional well-being."

- Cheryl Richardson

Day 48

Have you ever noticed that it's easy to absorb energy from the people around you? Surely you've had the experience of being around someone who made you feel exhausted or anxious. I bet you've had the opposite experience too, being around someone whose energy made you feel happy, energetic, and alive.

Energy transfers from one person to another. You can test positive today by intentionally choosing to surround yourself with people whose energy supports and magnifies your own.

Were you able to find someone whose energy helped magnify and support yours? Who?

_____

_____

How were you able to maintain your energy today? Did something happen to shift your energy?

_____

_____

"What you radiate outward
in your thoughts, feelings,
mental pictures and words,
you attract into your life."

- Catherine Ponder

Day 49

W hat you focus on most creates thought patterns in your mind, which will direct your energy in a specific way. Good or bad, it works the same. What you think about you bring about, because thoughts become things, so it's vital to be intentional about what you want and what thoughts dominate your mind.

The only way to attract the things you want in life is to BE the person who has those things. In other words, you don't attract what you want, you attract who you are. Decide how you want to feel and what you desire to experience. Don't allow anyone or anything to distract you.

What positive feelings and experiences do you plan to attract and experience today?

_____

_____

What was the outcome of intentionally directing your focus?

_____

_____

"Starve your distractions,
feed your focus."

- Unknown

Day 50

Today, let's test positive by taking personal responsibility. It's easy to blame others when you get distracted from your goals. "It's not my fault. It's because they….."

I say this with utmost respect, because we've all done it at one time or another, but if you ever think or say that, please know you're lying to yourself. The actions of others can affect you, but what they can't do is force you to give up. Remember it's your life, and no one has the power to permanently shape it. No one but you.

Focus on what you want and go get it. No distractions. No excuses. I believe in you.

How can you stay on track with your goals today?

_____

_____

What's a strategy you can use if someone distracts you from your goals? For example: your goal is to eat healthy, but your partner wants to go out for fast food?

_____

_____

"I don't think there's such a thing as a bad emotion. The only bad emotion is a stuck emotion."

- Rachel Naomi Remen

Day 51

Your issues live in your tissues. Specifically, the negative issues. When you latch on to negative emotions, and don't let go, it's possible they could manifest in your body as certain symptoms or illnesses.

Today, work on freeing yourself from any emotions that may be showing up as physical symptoms. For example, if you're having constant or recurrent stomach pain, maybe there's an emotional situation that you're having difficulty "digesting"? Or perhaps you have recurrent leg pain, a message from your tissues that you need to step forward or backward on an issue.

What issues might be living in your tissues?

_____

_____

What did you do to feel better? Did it work?

_____

_____

Our greatest
transformation happens
through our toughest times.

- Anna Pereira

Day 52

I f you find yourself complaining or talking about how awful things are during difficult times, remember that energy flows where your attention goes. It's okay to feel frustrated when things aren't going well, but focusing all of your attention on the negative can be harmful to your mental health.

A negative state of mind also affects you physiologically. Negative emotions will increase stress levels. Stress releases cortisol (often called "the stress hormone") which keeps your body in fight or flight mode. When this state is prolonged, it significantly detracts from your overall health. Testing positive doesn't mean wearing rose-colored glasses or living in denial. It means you've made the conscious choice to focus on the gifts of wisdom that may come from a difficult time. This is transformation.

What gifts have you received from difficult times in your life?

_____

_____

How can you shift your focus from complaining about a situation to the personal growth you'll experience as a result?

_____

_____

"The best day of your
life is the one on which you
decide your life is your own.
No apologies or excuses. No
one to lean on, rely on, or
blame. The gift is yours…"

- Bob Moawad

Day 53

I f you ask the most successful people in the world to share with you their secrets to success, at some point in the conversation they'll talk about intention, habits, and consistency.

What if, instead of waking up with no idea how your day will go, you decide ahead of time what it will be like?

Don't wait, create!

What are you creating for today?

_____

_____

After creating your intention, did the day go differently than it would've otherwise?

_____

_____

"The only person you should try to be better than, is the person you were yesterday."

- Matty Mullins

Day 54

If you'd like to avoid having a lousy day, don't get stuck in comparison! Comparing yourself to others is one of the easiest ways to begin feeling bad about yourself. Others may seem more attractive, successful, happy, or accomplished, but here's the thing that might surprise you; they probably look at you in the same way. Every person is unique and has their own strengths and weaknesses, so it isn't possible to draw an accurate comparison anyway.

Life isn't a competition, and the only person you should compare yourself to is the person you were yesterday. This isn't about being better than someone else, it's about your own personal growth. Testing positive today is about choosing to be a better version of yourself, not better than anyone around you.

What can you focus on today that'll lead you to a better version of yourself?

_____

_____

List two qualities you love that you see in someone you care about. Now, can you recognize that you possess those same qualities? We tend to love in others, what we ourselves possess.

_____

_____

"Respect your body
when it's asking for a break.

Respect your mind
when it's seeking rest.

Honor yourself when
you need a moment for yourself."

- Unknown

Day 55

Sometimes, testing positive means saying no. You can't be all things to all people all of the time,. If you try to stay "on" every moment, you're going to burn out. One of the people you have to say no to occasionally is you, because the voice in your head can be relentless. "You should be doing this," or "Why haven't you completed that?" There are times when you need to push hard, but there are times you must rest and recharge.

You can't pour from an empty cup, so listen to your body, tune in to your heart, and respect your own needs as much as you do the needs of others.

What does your heart and body need today?

_____

_____

What do you need to change or shift to make yourself a priority?

_____

_____

"Clutter is not just the stuff
on your floor, it's anything
that stands between you and
the life you want to be living"

- Peter Walsh

Day 56

They say, (whoever they are) "Clutter out, is clutter in." Okay, it might be me that says that. Anyway, the point is that a cluttered environment will make for a cluttered mind. The reverse is equally true, a cluttered mind creates a cluttered environment and life. Disorganization and clutter will have a cumulative effect on your brain. Your brain likes order, and disorganization causes anxiety and an inability to focus.

Today's a great day to deal with clutter—inside and out!

Where does the clutter in your life originate? Inside or outside?

_____

_____

What strategies can you use to reduce clutter, and regain control of your internal and external environments?

_____

_____

"Eyes forward. Mind focused.
Heart ready. Game on, world."

- Unknown

Day 57

R egardless of what today is, look ahead at the next seven days. Don't just let the next week happen. Set yourself up for success by designing it to your own specifications. Consider the most important areas of your life, and set some goals around them. Be intentional and access the power of attraction for what you want to happen during this timeframe.

If you want your life to change, YOU have to change it!

Set at least three goals for the next week.

How will you benefit from achieving these goals? How do you think you will feel?

"If it doesn't challenge
you, it won't change you.

- Fred DeVito

Day 58

Testing positive requires a growth mindset. If you want to be growth-focused, you have to choose opportunities to grow. Today's a great day to challenge yourself and get outside of your comfort zone. It takes some courage, but your greatest potential for personal growth happens when you're uncomfortable.

The only way limits can be placed on your growth is if you create them. If you've placed no such limits, then your expansion is without bounds.

How will you get out of your comfort zone today?

_____

_____

How will personal growth impact your quality of life?

_____

_____

When you complain, you make yourself into a victim. When you speak out, you are in your power. So change the situation by taking action or by speaking out if necessary or possible; leave the situation or accept it. All else is madness.

- Eckhart Tolle

Day 59

People often seem to love complaining about where they live. Whether it's about the government, healthcare, or weather, there's a never-ending list of unpleasantries.

The trouble with convincing yourself you're unhappy with where you're living is it keeps you in a negative frame of mind. I suppose you could move elsewhere, but are the problems actually contained within your specific locale, or is something else afoot? Could your mindset be the issue?

Today is a great day to challenge yourself to think of all the GOOD things about your town or home. Shifting to a positive outlook will release the feel-good hormones, and leave you feeling much lighter and happier.

List some of the reasons you chose to live in your current locale.

_____

_____

How can you shift your mindset about the place you call home?

_____

_____

"Decide what you won't compromise on in life and relationships. Then, don't."

- Doe Zantamata

Day 60

A re there things in your life you'd consider non-negotiable? Things you do for your own well-being and won't compromise on, no matter what? It's okay to make some compromises, but there are things upon which you should remain steadfast. For example, you may prioritize daily exercise because you place high value on health. However, when it's -40 outside you may decide not to go for a walk. You could keep your commitment to good health by going anyway, or choosing an indoor activity.

Honoring commitments to yourself is a solid way to test positive.

What commitment to yourself will you honor today?

_____

_____

What drives you to follow through on this commitment?

_____

_____

"Eat like you love yourself.
Move like you love yourself.
Speak like you love yourself.
Act like you love yourself."

- Unknown

Day 61

It isn't difficult to be good to people you love, but how good are you to yourself? It isn't sustainable to continue giving to others without taking the time to replenish your own heart and soul.

Today is a great day to treat yourself the way you'd treat a best friend!

What will you do today to spoil yourself a little?

_____

_____

How can you plan some regular "me" time to recharge?

_____

_____

"Do no harm and leave the world a better place than you found it."

- Patricia Cornwell

Day 62

One of my favorite things is collaborating with companies and coaching their employees. One concept I talk about is the importance of dealing with stress, and how to not trigger it in yourself and others.

Today's a great day to be gentle and kind with yourself, and every person you interact with. Build bridges instead of walls, and avoid being a source of distress. Bring peace into every situation. Start a ripple effect of kindness and observe the positive effect you'll have on others.

What are some typical stress triggers for you? How can you avoid them?

_____

_____

How were you able to bring calm and peace to others today?

_____

_____

Learn the art of saying "No."
Don't lie. Don't make excuses.
Don't over-explain yourself.
Just simply decline.

- Unknown

Day 63

It's time to test positive by letting go of your expectations for other people's expectations. When your gut says "No," honor yourself by listening. There's no reason to feel like you have to justify your boundaries. If it doesn't feel right, love and honor yourself enough to set boundaries that protect you from sacrificing your well-being in order to live up to other people's expectations.

Can you think of a time you sacrificed peace by trying to live up to someone else's expectations?

_____

_____

What boundaries do you need to create in order to protect your own well-being?

_____

_____

"When you're living in a different frequency and energetic vibration, a lot of times people can't hear and understand what you're saying. They can only meet you as deeply as they've met themselves. Don't drain your energy continually trying to explain yourself."

- Unknown

Day 64

A positive life is characterized by grace, kindness, and patience toward others. These traits make it possible to interact with others in such a way that they're affected in a positive way, but these traits are two-way streets.

What do I mean? I mean you should treat yourself the exact same way. You can't pour from an empty cup, nor can you treat others any differently than you treat yourself. Know when to share all of your energy, but also know when to pull back and recharge.

What are some ways you can demonstrate some grace, patience, and kindness toward someone today?

_____

_____

Is there anything preventing you from treating yourself in the same way? How can you change this?

_____

_____

"Remember an arrow can only be shot by pulling it backwards; so when you feel like life is dragging you down with difficulties, it simply means that it's going to launch you to something great. So just focus and keep aiming."

- Unknown"

Day 65

Here's a perfect way for you to test positive today: Know that whatever happens, you can handle it! Not only can you handle it, you're going to be better off because it happened. Life dishes out some tough and painful stuff sometimes, but getting through those times gives you wisdom and makes you more resilient.

If you're hurting today, you're not alone. I'm with you every step of the way, and together we'll keep moving forward.

Remember some tough times you overcame in the past. How did going through them make you stronger and wiser?

_____

_____

How can you use your experience to help others get through hard times?

_____

_____

"When you replace
'Why is this happening to me?'
with
'What is this trying to teach me?'

Everything shifts."

- Unknown

Day 66

We've all experienced it. Something unpleasant happens that makes us wonder, "Why me?" But what you may not realize is when you take that approach, it places you firmly in the role of the victim. When you take on that role, it's disempowering and seldom leads to a solution.

If you flip it and ask what the situation can teach you, you're no longer a victim and will be actively engaged in seeking a solution. It's choosing growth over stagnation. Now that's a great way to test positive!

Think of a time in the past when you assumed the victim role. How different would things have been if you had looked for the lesson?

_____

_____

How can you train yourself to do this more often?

_____

_____

"Life is 10% what happens to you
and 90% how you react to it."

- Charles R. Swindoll

Day 67

You've read today's quote before. You've heard it dozens of times. But has it taken root in your life? It's a gift to be able to choose your reactions every day. Remember, your issues live in your tissues, and if you allow other people or circumstances to create a negative emotional reaction, it's you who suffers the most.

You don't have to live in denial, because you can choose to react differently. With some practice, you'll be able to acknowledge the negative feelings and allow them to pass, which will result in a significant increase in your quality of life.

Today, consciously practice choosing your reactions to people and circumstances. How do you think it will affect your day?

_____

_____

At the end of the day, come back and write what you experienced.

_____

_____

"Being challenged in life is inevitable, being defeated is optional."

- Roger Crawford

Day 68

Contrary to what you've heard, it's okay to acknowledge it when things get tough. It isn't wrong to take some time and feel a little sorry for yourself—just don't stay there for long! Allow yourself to feel, let the emotions move through you, and then choose to move on.

Challenges in life are inevitable, but it's up to you whether or not you'll accept defeat.

Say this out loud, "I will not accept defeat!" How does that feel?

_____

_____

What was the last big challenge you faced? Did you accept defeat, or did you win by moving on?

_____

_____

"Focus on being productive
instead of busy."

- Tim Ferriss

Day 69

I'm a mother, friend, and entrepreneur, so believe it when I say I know what it's like to have a busy life. But, there's a huge difference between filling your time and filling your life. It's easy to schedule your days with tasks that keep you busy, but are those tasks actually moving you closer to the life you want to live, or are they distractions taking you further away?

Test positive today by concentrating the majority of your effort on productive things instead of things that just keep you occupied.

How would you describe your typical day? Busy or productive and what makes it so?

_____

_____

What tasks can you concentrate on today that'll move you closer to your ideal lifestyle?

_____

_____

"When life gives you
Monday, dip it in glitter and
sparkle all day."

- Ella Woodward

Day 70

Monday. Just the mention of it fills many people with a deep sense of dread. It signifies the beginning of the workweek, and the tug-of-war between work, family, leisure, and self-care. It doesn't even have to be Monday for those feelings to arise. You might feel that way on a Sunday evening, or in the middle of a week that seems like it'll never end. It isn't a fun way to live, but the good news is you can change it.

You can set the tone of your week (or day) by placing your focus on the reasons behind the things you do. Maybe that reason is your children, financial freedom, or a more meaningful life. Whatever your "why" might be, focus on it and sparkle today! If glitter and sparkle isn't your thing, just do something that makes today a little more fun and special.

What's your "why?" What keeps you going when things get hard?

_____

_____

What can you do to make today special?

_____

_____

"Joy is not a constant. It comes to us in moments– often ordinary moments. Sometimes we miss out on the bursts of joy because we're too busy chasing down the extraordinary moments."

- Brené Brown

Day 71

If there's one thing living through a global pandemic has taught me, it's that joy and happiness are often found in the moments in life we call ordinary.

There's so much beauty in creative expression, homemade meals, children, reading, alone time—simple things that are actually extraordinary.

What "ordinary" things do you find joy in every day?

_____

_____

What are some positive things you learned while living through a global pandemic?

_____

_____

"Friends are those rare people who ask how we are, and then wait to hear the answer."

- Ed Cunningham

Day 72

Good friends are vitally important for your mental health. Friendship offers shared life experiences, and so many opportunities to love and support. In other words, friends make life better! When you invest in those you love, and offer support without reservations or conditions, you enrich their lives as well as your own.

What do you love most about having good friends?

_____

_____

Make a point to reach out to your friends today. How can you support them right now?

_____

_____

"My dark days made me strong.
Or maybe I already was strong,
and they made me prove it."

- Emery Lord

Day 73

As a professional speaker, I frequently give presentations on surTHRIVING, which is about protecting your mental health and thriving during times of adversity. A critical skill that I emphasize is the ability to take a step back and realize that whatever you're facing, you're going to get through it. In fact, you've made it through 100% of every tough time you've ever faced. That's a pretty good track record.

Every obstacle you've faced, and every mountain you've climbed has made you stronger, more resilient, and capable.

You're unstoppable!

What are the things that make you unstoppable?

_____

_____

What strategies are you NOT using that you've wanted to explore like meditation, forest bathing, Qi Gong?

_____

_____

"Eating crappy food isn't a reward–it's a punishment."

- Drew Carey

Day 74

We're living in a time, and especially with social media, where people are intensely concerned with their looks and weight. It's as though image is everything, but I wish people would stop overthinking their image and start thinking about what they're putting into their bodies.

Think about it; you wouldn't pump hairspray into your car because it won't run on that. It needs the proper fuel, and the same is true for your body. If you don't feel healthy, look first at the kind of food you're eating. Love yourself enough to give your body what it needs to operate properly. That means whole foods, as close to their natural state as possible, and lots of vegetables. Skip the processed food too. You'll never regret making those choices!

Are there different food choices you could be making that would improve your health and well-being?

_____

_____

How do you think your current eating habits are affecting your health and energy levels?

_____

_____

"I can live for two months
on a good compliment."

- Mark Twain

Day 75

Today's a great day to give someone a heartfelt compliment! Compliments can be a form of influence and leadership, because people love to associate with individuals who are authentic and positive. It also encourages respect, gratitude, and open communication.

Some of my best friends have come from this simple act. I met one of my soul sisters after a "chance" (there are no coincidences in my opinion) meeting in the bathroom at a local farmers market, when I commented on how beautiful her hair looked. Make someone's day today, as well as your own, by offering heartfelt compliment.

Have you ever been the recipient of a heartfelt compliment? How did it make you feel?

_____

_____

Who is likely to cross your path today? Look for ways to offer a genuine compliment.

_____

_____

"Do what you love,
love what you do."

- Unknown

Day 76

I feel blessed that I get to work with businesses, and help their employees with important things like preventing injuries and creating healthy lifestyles. I teach them how to adopt proper ergonomics, and guide them through periods of intense stress that often manifests physically. I enjoy it so much that it truly doesn't feel like work. I love making a difference in the lives of others.

It's almost impossible to do anything long term, and remain happy, if you don't love doing it. Once you've identified what you love, and it fills your life with meaning, you'll look forward to waking up each day and living your purpose.

What do you love to do? Have you noticed it's usually something that has to do with serving others?

_____

_____

How can you narrow down to your "thing?" What clues do you notice in your life that indicate what you love to do?

_____

_____

"There are only two options: Make progress or make excuses."

- Tony Robbins

Day 77

It's human nature to want things to be easy. Your brain is wired to steer you in whichever direction requires the least amount of effort. Not because you're lazy, but because the brain's job is to keep you alive and safe—and it's simply too good at its job. The real work is doing what it takes in order to rewire your brain so that it recognizes nothing worthwhile comes without effort.

Today, you can test positive by rejecting excuses for why your life isn't going the way you want. It's within your power to change it, and you're the only one who holds that power. All you have to do is accept the responsibility and find one thing to change. After that, choose one more thing, and so on.

Do you remember a time you took the easy way instead of doing the work? How did things turn out?

_____

_____

What are some worthwhile things you want to accomplish? What actions must you take to get started?

_____

_____

"Because of your smile,
you make life beautiful."

- Thich Nhat Hanh

Day 78

You can improve someone's day by smiling. As a bonus, you'll make yourself feel better because your brain will release hormones to help you fight off stress. That's what I call a win/win situation! During the pandemic, I heard several people comment that others could no longer see them smile because of having to wear a mask. I reminded them that eyes can smile too! You've heard the expression, "The eyes are the window to the soul," and I believe that's true.

Have you noticed the way a person's eyes light up when they're smiling? It's unmistakable and beautiful. Go ahead and smile, mask or not, and let your light shine to others even if it's through your eyes. The world needs all the love it can get.

Have you ever had someone unexpectedly smile at you? How did it make you feel?

_____

_____

Offer a smile to everyone you interact with today. How did they react, and how was your day different?

_____

_____

"When you create a difference in someone's life, you not only impact their life, you impact everyone influenced by them throughout their entire lifetime. No act is ever too small. One by one, that is how to make an ocean rise."

- Danielle Doby

Day 79

You know there's much more to life than just taking what you can get. You're here to create love, happiness, and purpose. A powerful way to amplify these things in the world is by helping someone else. Why? Because by helping one person, you initiate a chain reaction, and a ripple effect that keeps going long afterwards. When a person has been helped by another, they automatically have the propensity to do the same for others.

Test positive today by creating waves of kindness, compassion, love and fun. If you change one moment for one person, you'll have done so for many more!

What are a few examples of the ripple effect you've personally experienced?

_____

_____

How can you initiate a positive chain reaction today?

_____

_____

"Miracles happen everyday,
change your perception of
what a miracle is and you'll
see them all around you."

- Jon Bon Jovi

Day 80

I'm waiting for a miracle. Have you ever heard or uttered those words? While I certainly understand the sentiment, the truth is you're surrounded by miracles every day. From the moment your eyes open in the morning, until you fall asleep at night, your day is filled with dozens of extraordinary things, but because they happen so often you call them "ordinary."

A sunrise, encouragement from a friend at just the right time, rain for your garden, a smile from a stranger—small miracles that make a huge difference in your life. You can test positive today by being a miracle for someone else, which is kind of a miracle in itself!

What are some "ordinary" things that are daily miracles for you?

_____

_____

How can you be a miracle for someone else today?

_____

_____

"See the light in others and treat them as if that's all you see."

- Wayne Dyer

Day 81

Respectfully, Up Yours! That's the title of a presentation I sometimes deliver to businesses. It's about creating a workplace environment that's characterized by respect, cooperation, and kindness. All these things affect your physical and mental health.

These are policies that speak to the heart, and not just the head. You may not love everyone you work with, and that's okay, but you can still treat them with kindness and respect. Honor the light that dwells within them, the same light that dwells in you.

Are there people in your workplace to whom you can show more kindness and respect?

_____

_____

How would a work environment based on cooperation and kindness affect you?

_____

_____

"You are in charge of how you react to the people and events in your life. You can either give negativity power over your life or you can choose happiness instead."

- Anais Nin

Day 82

Let's test positive today by intentionally choosing the kind of day or week we'll have. The way I see it, you have two options: You can wonder how things will go, or you can decide ahead of time. Even though you can't predict how every situation will unfold, you can decide what kind of mindset from which you'll respond.

Your thoughts can either limit or liberate you, so choose wisely!

How do you typically start a day or week? Do you decide your mindset ahead of time?

_____

_____

What kind of mindset do you need in order to make your day great?

_____

_____

"When we blame, we
give away our power."

- Greg Anderson

Day 83

It's easy to fall into blaming circumstances or people when things don't work out the way you wanted. Maybe you don't eat healthy because your spouse doesn't want to, so it's their fault. You don't enjoy your job because of a toxic co-worker, so it's their fault. You won't exercise regularly because you can't get time away from the kids, so it's their fault.

While any of those scenarios can be a genuine challenge, the final choice of whether you'll be a victim or victor lies with you. Test positive today by choosing to be a victor!

Can you remember a time when placing blame held you back?

_____

_____

How can you shift your perspective and accomplish the things you want to do?

_____

_____

"Whatever words we
utter should be chosen
with care for people will hear
them and be influenced by
them for good or ill."

- Unknown

Day 84

Have you heard of the 7-38-55 rule? It's a communication model developed by American psychologist, Albert Mehrabian. His model states that 7% of the meaning of feelings and attitudes comes through the words you use, 38% takes place through tone and voice, while 55% of communication takes place through body language—especially facial expressions. Wow! You see why things can go sideways when communicating through a text or email. Without tone and body language, much of what you write is open to the readers's interpretation.

Choose your words carefully, and try to convey your tone using emojis, symbols, or capital letters. In other words, BE MORE INTENTIONAL! See what I did there?

Have you ever had someone interpret a text or email incorrectly? What happened?

_____

_____

What are some other ideas to help you communicate effectively with others? Written or verbal.

_____

_____

"Love yourself enough to set boundaries. Your time and energy are precious. You get to choose how you use it. You teach people how to treat you by deciding what you will and won't accept."

- Anna Taylor

Day 85

Would you like to test positive today? Of course you do! Then ask yourself, "What am I teaching others about how I wish to be treated?" That's right, people learn how to treat you based on what you accept from them. In other words, what you permit, you promote. If people are treating you with disrespect, abuse, or manipulation, it could be because you've allowed it to happen in the past.

Training others how to behave toward you starts with some self-awareness. The way you treat yourself sets the standard for others on how you wish to be treated. You deserve the best, from yourself as well as others.

How do you feel you are treated by most people in your life?

_____

_____

Can you see how you might have trained others to treat you in a certain way by accepting or allowing certain behaviors?

_____

_____

"Be the person that makes others feel special. Be known for your kindness and grace."

- Unknown

Day 86

L et's test positive today by helping others feel better! It seems as though some people wake up in the morning and decide to have a crappy day. They might not do it consciously, but the result is the same.

Be on the lookout today for people who seem to be struggling, suffering, or just having a bad day, and go out of your way to be graceful and kind. Oftentimes, that's all it takes to make them feel better and turn their day around.

Have you been on the receiving end of someone's kindness and it made your whole day better? Write about the experience.

_____

_____

What can you do today to improve someone else's bad day?

_____

_____

"Personal resilience softens
the impact of abrupt change,
and shortens the recovery time
when hardship occurs."

- Gregg Braden

Day 87

Personal resilience is something I've worked on for years. When you're able to withstand and recover quickly from difficult situations, setbacks become set ups for something better, chaos is replaced with order, and surviving transforms into thriving. It doesn't mean you'll no longer experience anger, grief, or trauma. It means you allow those things to move through you, rather than being stuck inside of you where they could end up making you sick.

The good news is that resilience can be learned through developing thoughts and behaviors that'll help you recover from traumatic or stressful events.

On a scale of 1-10 (10 being the highest) how resilient are you?

_____

_____

What actions can you take to help you become more resilient?

_____

_____

"Start by doing one push up. Start by drinking one cup of water. Start by paying toward one debt. Start by reading one page. Start by making one sale. Start by deleting one old contact. Start by walking one lap. Start by attending one event. Start today. Repeat tomorrow.

- Unknown

Day 88

I f you feel like there's room for improvement in your life, you might be struggling with where and how to begin. Change can be overwhelming at times, but you can make it a bit easier by taking one step at a time.

Maybe you'd like to eat healthier, exercise, be more productive, finish that project, make a sale, or start a business. It might be all of those things, but you can test positive today by choosing to take just one small step. That's all it takes to help reduce the psychic clutter and get you moving toward your goals!

Which areas of your life do you want to change or improve?

_____

_____

What's one step you can take today toward one of your goals?

_____

_____

"Sometimes the most important thing in a whole day is the rest we take between two deep breaths."

- Etsy Hillesum

Day 89

Some days, living through a global pandemic feels like the weight of the world is resting on my shoulders. Have you experienced similar feelings? We're all surrounded by chaos, fear, and highly-charged emotions, and that kind of vibrational energy feels heavy and dark.

However, you don't have to sit under all that weight. When you're being bombarded with negativity it's time to take action. Fast from negative people, crappy food, the news, and anything else that causes you distress. The prescription for testing positive today is a double dose of self-care and self-love. Rest, breathe, and surround yourself everything and everyone that makes your heart happy!

What can you do to deal with the people or things in your life that are causing you distress?

_____

_____

What can you fast from in order to bring peace and well-being back into your life?

_____

_____

"One day, you'll look back and realize that you worried too much about things that didn't really matter."

- Unknown

Day 90

Do you occasionally find yourself overcome with worry about something? I know I do, and I've done it enough to know that worrying has never helped me in any situation. It doesn't change the outcome, and it's harmful to my physical and mental health.

Whatever you're going through in this moment, please know that it will pass. You've made it through every tough situation you've ever been in, and you'll get through this one too. Worry takes you out of the present moment and puts your energy onto something in the future that may never happen. Keep your focus on the present reality, the only thing that currently matters, and worry will fade away.

In what way has worry been stealing your focus and energy away from the present?

_____

_____

Can you remember a time you worried yourself sick, and later realized it was for no reason?

_____

_____

"I'm not just a dreamer, I'm a hope-aholic."

- Gloria Steinem

Day 91

I've read some disturbing statistics on how alcoholism, food and shopping addictions, and more, have increased due to the global pandemic. Maybe it's about time for us to get addicted to hope, which has nothing to do with denial and everything to do with our ability to handle whatever comes our way.

When you possess hope, you have the belief that a better future is possible and that you have a role to play in bringing it about. It helps make tough situations more bearable, and can also improve your life because envisioning a better future motivates you to take the steps to make it happen.

Do you believe a better future is possible? Why?

_____

_____

What steps can you take to help bring it about??

_____

_____

"If you avoid conflict to
keep the peace, you start
a war inside yourself."

- Cheryl Richardson

Day 92

It's a sobering truth, but life will never be completely free of conflicts. That's just a fact. You can attempt to avoid them by ignoring what's wrong, but that never ends well.

It might feel counterintuitive, but in order to live a positive life you must honor your truth and speak it whenever necessary. You can do this without being a jerk. Respectfully dealing with conflict builds bridges, prevents walls of resentment, anger, and fear from ever being built.

Have you avoided conflicts in the past? What was the outcome?

_____

_____

What are some available avenues you can take to respectfully deal with conflict in your life?

_____

_____

"She was unstoppable. Not because she didn't have failures or doubts, but because she continued on despite them."

- Beau Taplin

Day 93

If you believe that you're here for a purpose, nothing will stand in your way. When you know beyond a shadow of a doubt that the goal of making the world a better place is definitely within reach, you become unstoppable.

Everything you encounter in life has the potential to help you grow and develop into the kind of person who refuses to live life from a place of fear, anger, or hopelessness. Keep your heart and mind open, and live from a place of hope, healing, and gratitude. You'll experience more happiness and joy, while influencing others for good. Who doesn't want more of that?

What's your purpose, the work you know you're here to do?

_____

_____

What's happening in your life right now that's molding you into a more effective world-changer?

_____

_____

"People don't want to be
talked out of their feelings.
People want to be heard,
seen, felt, and understood."

- Rachel Samson

Day 94

I've noticed that many people think I'm happy and positive all of the time. Although that's mostly true, I experience the same emotions as everyone else. I deal with fear, frustration, grief, and all the rest. I'm positive most of the time, not because I live in denial of those feelings, but because of how I manage them. How do I do it? I've found that meditation and talking about my feelings with the people I trust helps me a lot. I use both of these tactics to help me acknowledge and release the emotions.

Denial of your emotions (or suppressing them) just bottles them all up, which means they'll come back with a vengeance at some point in the future. Your feelings are valid. They deserve to be seen and heard, and then they deserve to be set free.

What feelings are you experiencing today?

_____

_____

Have you tried meditation? Who is your trusted confidant that you can talk to about how you're feeling?

_____

_____

"Today I close the door to the past, open the door to the future, take a deep breath, step on through and start a new chapter in my life."

- Louise L. Hay

Day 95

very day is an opportunity to write a brand new chapter in your life. No matter what's happening, if you don't like the way things are going, you can change the story and create a different outcome.

If there's something holding you down, you can test positive today by letting go of it and grabbing onto a new perspective. It's your story after all, and you're holding the pen!

If today appears to be headed in a negative direction, how can you write a different ending?

_____

_____

What outcome would you love to write for the end of the day, week, month?

_____

_____

"Develop enough courage
so that you can stand up
for yourself and then stand
up for somebody else."

- Maya Angelou

Day 96

I grew up in an abusive home. As a result, I developed a conflict phobia, know what I mean? For years, I'd go to extremes in order to avoid conflict. The problem with trying to avoid all conflict is that you end up compromising your own feelings and bottling up frustration which will negatively affect your physical and mental health.

I've spent the last several years putting forth a ton of intentional effort into properly dealing with conflict. It takes a lot of work, and even more courage, but you can do it too. It's time to test positive by showing up for yourself, and anyone else who needs a friend in their corner.

How do you manage conflict? Do you avoid it, or deal with it appropriately?

_____

_____

Think of the last time you experienced conflict. How did you resolve it? Or did you?

_____

_____

"At the end of the
day, the only questions
I will ask myself are:
Did I love enough?
Did I laugh enough?
Did I make a difference?"

- Katrina Mayer

Day 97

When it comes to self care, you may think it sounds a bit counterintuitive to consider helping others as a way to help yourself, but it really works! You've heard the expression, "It's better to give than receive," but did you know it's backed up by research?

Evidence has shown that helping others benefits your well-being and mental health. It helps reduce stress, improves self-esteem, and makes you happier. Plus, it reminds you of your true purpose. You have the power to help yourself and others. Can you imagine a world where we all did that?

Do you remember a time when helping someone made you feel better?

_____

_____

Who made a difference in YOUR life today?

_____

_____

"Don't be too hard on yourself. There are plenty of people willing to do that for you. Love yourself and be proud of everything that you do. Even mistakes mean you're trying."

- Susan Gale

Day 98

If you're like me, you probably demand a lot from yourself. You push hard to accomplish goals, and when you do it's on to the next one. When you don't achieve your goal, you come down hard on yourself. Sound familiar?

It's time to test positive by no longer beating yourself up! Leave the past where it is, and let go of your regrets. It's good to accept responsibility for your life, but instead of allowing mistakes to derail you, learn from them and move on. No need to place blame or be a victim—both of these things hurt and hold you down. Every shot you take is more than many people will attempt. Be proud of where you are and what you've accomplished so far!

What's the most recent mistake you remember? What did you learn from it?

_____

_____

What are at least five things you're proud to have accomplished?

_____

_____

"May you have the
courage to break the
patterns in your life that
are no longer serving you."

- Unknown

Day 99

If you want your life to change, then you have to change it. When you continue in patterns of negative thinking, nothing will move in the right direction. Sometimes, what you need is a serious pattern interrupt to shake you up and out of a life stuck on autopilot.

Example: In the presence of aggressive and controlling people you become passive and compliant. Does that serve you? Definitely not! A bold pattern interrupt would be to set clear boundaries, or maybe even ending a relationship. If nothing changes, then nothing changes. There are few things more liberating than breaking old patterns that have been holding you back.

Spend time in deep reflection. Can you recognize any patterns that are no longer serving you?

_____

_____

What are some bold pattern interrupts you can take action on?

_____

_____

"There is no exercise better for
the heart than reaching down
and lifting people up."

- John Holmes

Day 100

You can test positive today by being there for others when they need you. Being "there" means being present in the moment, listening and holding space for someone who needs your help or simply an ear. With practice, you'll even begin to anticipate what others need before they voice it.

Asking for help is one of the hardest things to do, so when you see a need, offer to fill it whether they ask or not. All it takes is a willing heart filled with love and fueled by compassion.

How does it make you feel when someone is there for you when needed?

_____

_____

What holds you and others back from reaching out for help during a struggle?

_____

_____

"There's very few people go the extra mile - so go the extra mile and give it all you've got."

– Jim Leishman

Day 101

Have you ever received service that was over the top, and was beyond your highest expectations? I bet you came away from that experience filled with gratitude, and that you were valued and appreciated. It's a wonderful feeling!

How about testing positive today by giving that same experience to everyone you interact with today? Going the extra mile doesn't cost you anything, but the rewards are priceless. Be intentional with this today, raise your own vibration and begin a ripple effect of kindness. I believe you'll find that you'll attract more of the same into your own life.

What can you do today that'll help give someone the feeling of being appreciated and valued?

_____

_____

How did going above and beyond for someone else make you feel?

_____

_____

"People inspire you,
or they drain you.
Pick them wisely."

- Hans F. Hasen

Day 102

Sometimes, we make excuses for allowing the energy drainers in our lives to take up so much time and space. "That's just how they are," or "I don't let it bother me," are thinly veiled indicators that you're being affected in a negative way.

You don't always have to boot someone completely out of your life, but you do have to protect your energy or risk being pulled down with them. Limit the time you hang around such people, and increase the amount of time you spend with people who inspire you to be your best.

What excuses have you made excuses for the energy drainers in your life?

_____

_____

Who in your life inspires you to be your very best?

_____

_____

"The best times in life are
usually random, unplanned,
and completely spontaneous."

- Unknown

Day 103

As an entrepreneur, I know the value of having a schedule, and make good use of my time. However, there are times when spontaneity, flexibility, and disrupting my routines is exactly what I need.

When you were a child, being spontaneous was natural, but people tend to move away from that as they get older and take on more responsibility. I say it's time to tap into your inner child and bring back the fun that comes with spur-of-the-moment fun!

When was the last time you did something fun and spontaneous?

_____

_____

What can you do today to change things up?

_____

_____

"Always ask yourself if what you're doing today is getting you closer to where you want to be tomorrow."

- Paulo Coelho

Day 104

It's easy to complain about what you don't have or that things aren't going your way. Instead of complaining, ask yourself if you're taking the necessary steps to bring about change. Even baby steps toward your goal, when taken consistently, will achieve what you desire the most!

No matter what may appear on the surface, no one in history has ever made a significant change in their life without taking action Consistent commitment is the key. Test positive today by taking just one step in the direction of your goal.

What's the most important goal you want to achieve?

_____

_____

What's one step you can take today?

_____

_____

"I am thankful for all
those difficult people in
my life, they have shown me
exactly who I do not want to be."

- Unknown

Day 105

Holding on to bitterness and anger toward someone who hurt you affects you more than them. I know it isn't easy, but you could choose to feel grateful for the experience because it pushed you to become a better person and demonstrated how not to be.

An abusive boss may push you to create stronger boundaries, a toxic relationship may help you raise your standards. These kinds of experiences are painful, but they can be instrumental in your own healing and strengthen your resolve. Test positive today by letting go of pain and anger. Instead, embrace gratitude for who you've become!

Have you been holding on to anger and hurt? How will it feel to finally let go?

_____

_____

Why is letting go hard?

_____

_____

"Your body is a temple for your mind, body, and soul. So nourish it with only happy thoughts good health, and positive energy."

- Unknown

Day 106

Your body is a temple, and today's a wonderful day to test positive by treating it like one! Show some gratitude and reverence for your body by choosing high-quality, whole foods along with lots of veggies. Get moving and hit the gym, go for a walk, or bicycle ride.

Be your own best friend and spoil yourself with some extra self-care and happy thoughts. You might be surprised at how far you can go when you show yourself some extra love.

When was the last time you showed your body a little TLC?

_____

_____

What are three things you can do today to care for your body?

_____

_____

"No one can ever make you feel bad, mad, or sad without your cooperation!"

- Unknown

Day 107

D o you ever find yourself saying that someone made you mad or feel bad? I know I have, but the truth is that I allowed it to happen. At one time or another, we've all blamed someone else for our hurt feelings, but no one can literally "make" you feel anything. Their words and actions may trigger you, but they cannot force you to feel a certain way.

It may feel defeating to realize you're responsible for how you feel, but it's actually great news because your mindset is something you can control! That means you don't have to wallow in those negative feelings, you can choose your way out. Here's how you can test positive today: If someone does or says anything that triggers negative feelings, shift your perspective by pausing for a couple of deep breaths to give yourself space for a thoughtful response.

How have you been triggered into some negative feelings recently?

_____

_____

How can you shift your mindset and turn things around?

_____

_____

"Starve your distractions.
Feed your focus."

- Unknown

Day 108

When you know your day is going to be busy, it's easy to get distracted and not accomplish everything you set out to do. One reason that occurs is your brain feels overwhelmed. When that happens, distractions offer a brief respite from the to-do list, thus creating a seductive trap! You can avoid this by keeping your focus squarely on your goals. Narrow your focus down to one thing at a time, and you can avoid overwhelm too.

When you set your intention at the beginning of the day, don't be surprised when your day goes exactly the way you planned!

What has distracted from your goals recently?

_____

_____

What strategy can you use to stay laser-focused on your goals?

_____

_____

"If everything around
seems dark, look again,
you may be the light."

- Rumi

Day 109

We all know what it's like to experience a rough day, and then have someone show us a little kindness, love, and compassion. It's life-changing!

Being there for others, even when you're struggling, helps you as much as it does them. The gift of kindness, love and compassion has the capacity to change the giver as well as the receiver. Giving to others is not only a beautiful distraction from your own struggle, it also enhances your health. Another win/win situation!

Is there someone you know who needs some love, kindness, and compassion today? How can you share these things with them?

_____

_____

How does it feel knowing you have changed someone's day for the better?

_____

_____

"We cannot cure the world of sorrows, but we can choose to live in joy."

- Joseph Campbell

Day 110

Testing positive is really about shifting your energy. What you radiate, you will attract. The emotions of love, joy and compassion are higher vibrational emotions and will attract experiences to keep that high vibration going. The opposite is also true.

Today is a great day to shift your energy and focus on those high frequency beautiful emotions!

How can you bring the energy of love, compassion, and kindness into your day?

_____

_____

How did focusing on these high-vibe emotions affect your day?

_____

_____

"Anyone can find the dirt in someone. Be the one who finds the gold."

- Proverbs 11:27

Day 111

Have you noticed how easy it can be to find fault in people around you, even people you don't know? Why is that? I've found that it's often because we don't feel good about ourselves, so we project those negative feelings onto others.

Test positive today by looking for the "gold" in others. If someone rubs you the wrong way, say to yourself, "Someone loves them. I wonder what it is about them that's lovable?" Be curious instead of judgmental!

How can you find pieces of "gold" in someone who annoys you today?

_____

_____

What is it about you that others might find annoying?

_____

_____

"I learned that courage was
not the absence of fear, but
the triumph over it."

- Nelson Mandela

Day 112

Did you know fear is usually the driver behind negative emotions like anger, irritation, or self-doubt? If you don't manage your fears, they'll end up managing you. You can test positive today by intentionally choosing courage and doing the hard things. When you face it head-on, fear will lose its power over you. That brings freedom, and freedom is priceless!

What fears do you most often experience?

_____

_____

In what way are you willing to confront and deal with those fears today?

_____

_____

"It is not joy that makes us grateful; it is gratitude that makes us joyful."

- David Steindl-Ras

Day 113

Don't you love how infectious joy is? And being around joyful people is so amazing and fun. They're like magnets and so attractive! No matter what you're going through, gratitude is your path back to joy. There's always something to be grateful for.

Would you like to test positive today? Tap into gratitude and create some joy!

What are some things you're grateful for that bring you joy?

_____

_____

What can you do today to protect your joy? For example, do you need to avoid the news or stay away from negative people?

_____

_____

She picked her head
up and the angles cried,
"You are going to save lives."

- Unknown

Day 114

Have you been so down in the dumps, or burdened, that you found yourself desperately praying for an angel, someone to lean on, and help lift you up? Of course you have!

What if someone in your life today is feeling just like that? What if you could be their angel and an answer to their prayers?

How can you be the answer to someone's prayer today?

_____

_____

What help do YOU need, and can you ask for it?

_____

_____

"Be crazy, be stupid, be silly, be weird. Be whatever, because life is too short to be anything but happy."

- Unknown

Day 115

Today, testing positive is all about fun! It's time to let go, put aside what you cannot control, and not take everything so seriously. Give yourself, and others, a break today and have some fun! When you choose to have fun, you receive the added bonus of a healthier body.

Laughter really is the best medicine!

How can you give yourself a break today and have some fun?

_____

_____

What can you do to lighten the mood at home or work?

_____

_____

"Let your smile change the world, but don't let the world change your smile."

- Connor Franta

Day 116

L et's start the day strong by using today's quote as a mantra to guide you through the day. It's one of my favorite quotes, and my friends and family hear me say it often. I feel so strongly about it that it's included in a presentation I frequently deliver to businesses.

Starting a day with intention is a powerful way to create your day, rather than waiting to see what happens. Don't wait when you can create! You'll attract more of what you want and accomplish more too.

What is your favorite mantra that helps create your day? If you don't have one, create one!

_____

_____

How does starting your day like this affect the outcome?

_____

_____

"Let it hurt. Let it bleed.

Let it heal. And let it go."

- Nikita Gill

Day 117

Courage. That's what it takes to allow yourself to experience your emotions, especially when they're painful. Whatever you're feeling at any given moment is valid and should be acknowledged. You could suppress it, or try ignoring it, but it will surface again. It's okay to experience your feelings and allow them to move through you. Otherwise, they may show up in physical ways, which is why I often say, "Your issues live in your tissues."

Be courageous today by facing your feelings instead of seeking an escape or distraction. Talk to someone about the way you feel and claim your power over your emotions by letting go.

What issues are you struggling with?

_____

_____

How can you move past your negative emotional energy? What strategy will you use to stop these issues from settling into your tissues?

_____

_____

"Hurt people, hurt people. That's how pain patterns get passed on, generation after generation after generation. Break the chain today. Forgive and forget about finding fault. Love is the weapon of the future."

- Yehuda Berg

Day 118

I'm sure you're familiar with the expression, "Hurt people, hurt people," but were you aware that healed people, heal people? It's a beautiful truth. Another truth is you don't have to be completely healed in order to help someone, because helping others is one way you heal yourself. Isn't that incredible?

You can also further your healing by dialing back your reaction toward the person who caused you emotional pain. Pause for just a moment and consider what they must've been through in order to become the kind of person that lashes out at others. Their behavior probably has nothing at all to do with you, but is rooted in a past experience in their own life. That doesn't excuse their behavior, but it does help you to not take it personally.

What explanation can you find for some of the hurtful behavior that you have experienced from others?

_____

_____

What can you do today to move towards healing?

_____

_____

"I had to make you uncomfortable, otherwise, you never would have moved."

- Universe

Day 119

I get goosebumps when I read today's quote. I've lived the truth of that statement many times. It's like sitting in a chair for a long time, and your body becomes very uncomfortable. After all, your body wasn't designed to maintain that unhealthy posture for long periods of time. How do you resolve the situation? You get up and move. Almost instantly, you feel better because your body needs to move.

The same is true for your life. When living a certain way becomes uncomfortable, or you feel like you're stuck, it's time to move! It's time to change things and trust that the Universe will have your back.

What is making you uncomfortable and holding you back from moving forward on something that's important to you?

_____

_____

How will moving forward on this affect your quality of life? What would be different?

_____

_____

"Look back at where you came from and let yourself feel proud about your progress."

- Unknown

Day 120

D o you ever find yourself getting so caught up in your to-do list that you forget your "have done" list? Today, testing positive is about focusing on how far you've come. It's easy to become consumed by what you want to do and forget that you've accomplished so much already.

Celebrate your wins, not just material achievements, but the deeper things like personal growth, peace, forgiveness, and love. Now that's progress!

What is on your "have done" list? Take time to celebrate!

_____

_____

Which accomplishment are you most proud of, and why?

_____

_____

"A change in bad habits leads
to a change in life."

- Jenny Craig

Day 121

Would you like test positive today, and move toward your highest potential at the same time? Unload some bad habits! Research has shown that creating new routines, and sticking with them until they become habits, will transform your life.

If the last few years have led you to develop habits that are holding you down, it's time to replace them with habits that'll lift you up.

What habits are holding you back from living the life you want?

_____

_____

Start with one negative habit. What positive routine can you begin to replace it?

_____

_____

"Obstacles are the cost of greatness."

- Robin Sharma

Day 122

I f you're going through a tough time, consider that you have a perfect track record of overcoming every mountain that's ever been in your path. How many times have you wondered if you could go on, but you did? All those times are in the past which is proof that you did it!

You're exceptional at solving problems. How do I know? Because you've solved every problem that has stood in your way so far. You might need a helping hand every now and then, but you always find a way. This time will be no exception. Over it, under it, around or through it, you're going to make it—just like you always do.

What mountain seems impossible to overcome right now?

_____

_____

Who or what can help you find the courage to scale this mountain?

_____

_____

"When you start seeing your worth, you'll find it harder to stay around people who don't."

- Unknown

Day 123

A re there people in your life who tend to be negative and needy? Do they drag you down? It's hard to test positive around those kinds of people. Sometimes we keep people like that in our lives because we don't value ourselves enough to set limits with people who steal our joy and drain all of our energy. If you continue devaluing yourself, you'll keep attracting people who also devalue you.

Today, focus on self-love. Shift your energy and accept your true value and see what you attract!

What's keeping you from disconnecting with negative people?

_____

_____

What steps can you take to create boundaries with people who are negative energy drainers?

_____

_____

"Being safe is about being
seen and heard and allowed
to be who you are and to
speak your truth."

- Rachel Naomi Remen

Day 124

Few things hurt more than sharing what's in your heart only to have someone invalidate or dismiss your feelings. It's like they don't care, or that your feelings are unimportant.

Let's test positive today by being there for someone else, making them feel seen and heard. Give them the gift of being themselves without being judged by another.

While you're at it be sure to treat yourself the same way. Too often we dismiss our own thoughts by saying "It could be worse." There are times when that may be appropriate but pause a moment and acknowledge that your feelings are valid before letting them go. Remember, our issues live in our tissues, but only if we allow it.

How can you be present for someone today? How can you validate and care for them?

_____

_____

In what ways can you be present for yourself?

_____

_____

"Happiness is not something ready-made. It comes from your own actions."

- Dalai Lama

Day 125

If you've ever said, "I'd be happy if—it doesn't matter what you said after "if" but whatever it may be, that's the reason you're unhappy. You can't test positive if you've made your happiness contingent upon anything outside of yourself.

It doesn't matter what job you have, where you live, or who you're with, because happiness is always an inside job!

In what ways do you sabotage your own happiness?

_____

_____

What can you do today to create authentic happiness?

_____

_____

t

"Remember your divinity, your authentic self. For it is all that you are, all that you'll ever be."

- Unknown

Day 126

Always remember that you are a divine creature having an earthly experience. This isn't about religion, it's about the knowledge that you're a spiritual being and love is your currency. You're not only capable of experiencing the divine, but also sharing it with others through connection.

Connection is a basic human need, and it has the magical ability to change lives!

What are a few ways you can use the currency of love today?

_____

_____

How can you create a deep connection with someone in whose presence you feel safe and loved?

_____

_____

"Life has no meaning. Each of us has meaning and we bring it to life. It is a waste to be asking the question when you are the answer."

- Joseph Campbell

Day 127

Have you discovered your purpose? What's your reason for being on the planet at this moment in time? Purpose is very often connected to passion. What lights you up, and makes you feel like you're making a difference in the world? Pay close attention because those are clues to your purpose.

Finding your purpose makes life worth living, and you don't have to go out looking for it. It's already inside of you!

What lights you up and makes life meaningful for you?

_____

_____

How does it feel to live out your purpose? How can you connect to it even deeper?

_____

_____

"Quitting is ok if you're quitting something that's slowly killing you so you can step into something that will give you life."

- Tony Gaskins

Day 128

How many people quit before reaching the finish line? You don't win if you don't finish. You can test positive today by following through on what you've started. If you get tired, take a break. Just don't give up.

Naturally, there's a flip side to this. There will be times when you need to quit something (or someone) in order to step away from what's hurting you, and into something that gives you life.

What have you given up on too soon? Is it time for you to start again?

_____

_____

What or whom do you need to quit?

_____

_____

"In the end, we only regret the chances we didn't take, the relationships we were afraid to have, and the decisions we waited too long to make."

- Lewis Carroll

Day 129

I'm guilty of having allowed fears to paralyze me. At various times in my life, I've allowed them to hold me back. However, I've discovered that when I take bold and courageous action, I never regret it!

Today is a great day to take a chance, move forward on something you've been fearful about, and follow your heart.

How has fear been holding you back?

_____

_____

Are there bold decisions you could make, or any actions you can take that'll move you forward?

_____

_____

"Energy is contagious:
either you affect people
or you infect people."

- T. Harv Eker

Day 130

We're often observers of our own emotional and spiritual energy. We say things like, "I have no energy today" as if it's something that happens outside of our control. In fact, you control, create, and impact others with your energy. It begins with your mindset and the direction of your thoughts.

Test positive today by focusing your energy on creating gratitude, love, abundance, and generosity. You attract things into your life, not because of what you want, but because of who you are.

How can you share love, gratitude, abundance, or generosity today?

_____

_____

What can you do to protect yourself from negative energy?

_____

_____

"Forgive others, not because they deserve forgiveness, but because you deserve peace."

- Jonathan Lockwood Huie

Day 131

W e've all had someone treat us poorly or cause our loved ones to experience pain. The question is whether you've let it go. Holding on to pain will not only harm you emotionally, it'll also manifest physically. No one suffers more than you when you hang on to anger or bitterness.

Chances are that there's someone out there who has forgiven you. Can you do the same for someone else? It doesn't matter if they deserve it or not, because you do.

Who do you need to forgive?

_____

_____

What do you need to forgive yourself for?

_____

_____

"The world exists
as you perceive it.
It is not what you
see, it is how you see it.
It is not what you
hear, but how you hear it.
It is not what you
feel, but how you feel it."

- Rumi

Day 132

Y ou already know that it isn't about what happens to you in life, but how you respond to it. The choice rests with you. I had a client who got very angry with herself for arriving late to an event due to her intense anxiety about not being able to find a parking spot. She perceived that as a failure on her part. I saw it as an incredible win over her anxiety. In spite of her anxiety and being late, she went anyway!

Test positive today and focus on how you're perceiving the world around you. How do you see, hear, and feel?

What aspect of your life can you choose to see differently, or more positively?

_____

_____

What helps you dial down negative reactions and gain perspective?

_____

_____

"The real trick in life is to turn hindsight into foresight that reveals insight."

- Robin S. Sharma

Day 133

Hindsight Hindsight brings much needed clarity to something that, at the time it happened, you didn't completely understand. It may have been the loss of a job, and months or years later you could see how it led to a better opportunity. Perhaps it was the end of a relationship, and after time had passed, it became easy to see you were being undervalued.

What if you could use the gift of hindsight in the present moment? What if you could look at your current situation and ask yourself, "Six months from now, what potential good will I think came from this?" It's a simple, yet powerful, shift in perspective that may give you insight into the present moment. You might even improve the situation. Positive energy attracts more of the same!

What are three possible gifts that may come from the challenge you're experiencing right now?

_____

_____

What's the best thing that came from the worst thing you've lived through?

_____

_____

"Sometimes you don't realize the weight of something you've been carrying until you feel the weight of it's release."

- Unknown

Day 134

Testing positive today is about releasing the weight of what you've been carrying. Excess emotional baggage weighs on more than just your mind, it also affects your body.

In certain kinds of health practices, chronic lower back pain can be a sign of emotional trauma that has not been released. Pain in your legs may be about not stepping forward into a decision or stepping into a decision you shouldn't have. Your body is affected by your emotional experiences. Anger, unforgiveness, resentment, fear—these things must be released. If you don't, symptoms may show up in your body that force you to pay attention. Once you've let go of that weight, you'll be amazed at how much better you feel!

What trauma or negative emotions have you been holding on to?

_____

_____

What symptoms are you currently experiencing? They may be messages from your mindbody.

_____

_____

"Throw out old clothes and shoes, and train your brain to get rid of old thoughts and ideas."

- Karen Salmansohn

Day 135

You can test positive today by throwing out the trash—including any mental garbage that has been piling up! All the things that don't serve you, hurt you, and keep you small. It all needs to go.

Choose things that are holding you back. Old beliefs, behaviors, and stories you've carried with you since childhood. If anyone has said you're not smart enough, strong enough, successful enough, or pretty enough, and you believed it, toss it all into the dumpster. Someone else's opinion of you is not the real story. You get to decide that, and when you do, you'll experience true freedom.

What's a story or belief you've held onto that does not serve you and may not be true?

_____

_____

How will your life change when you finally let it go?

_____

_____

"Life's most persistent and
urgent question is, 'What
are you doing for others?'"

- Martin Luther King, Jr.

Day 136

Many people had to make incredible sacrifices in order for us to enjoy a life of security and freedom. What are you willing to sacrifice for the peace and freedom of others? We're not here for ourselves alone, we're here to walk each other home. Test positive today by reflecting on how you can support the health, safety, and well-being of everyone.

How can you support the people you love in terms of their health, safety, and well-being?

_____

_____

In what ways can you focus on supporting your own health, safety, freedom, and well-being?

_____

_____

"Our bodies communicate to us clearly and specifically, if we are willing to listen to them."

- Shakti Gawain

Day 137

How often do you feel tired, sore, sad, or mad, and ignore it? It's easy to dismiss, or not pay attention, to what's going on with your body, but symptoms are the language your body uses to speak to you! For example, chronic headaches might be a sign of overthinking. Lower back pain could be the result of emotional trauma that hasn't been dealt with. Arm or shoulder pain just might be signs of carrying too much emotional baggage.

Pay attention to your body, and its symptom language, because it's trying is trying to tell you something. Your life may depend on it!

Do you have any reoccurring symptoms that appeared without a specific trigger? It could be a communication about something that needs to be released.

_____

_____

What strategy will you use to release this emotional bond?

_____

_____

"You don't always have to be strong. Sometimes you need to scream, cuss throw shit, or have a really good cry. But you always, always, always, need to pull yourself back together, then go back to being the badass you were meant to be."

- Unknown

Day 138

Testing positive doesn't mean you only see the bright side of everything. It means you acknowledge what you're feeling, and then release negative emotions. It takes more courage to acknowledge negative feelings than it does to suppress them and pretend you're fine. I can't overemphasize that your issues live in your tissues.

If you're struggling, talk about it with someone you trust, go for a walk, exhale the negative energy, and have the courage to feel it. Then get on with the business of creating a beautiful day.

What negative feelings do you need to acknowledge today?

_____

_____

Work at releasing your negative feelings. How does doing that change things for you?

_____

_____

"Giving up is hard.
Pushing through the
struggle is hard.
Choose your hard."

- Unknown

Day 139

The well-known philanthropist and wealthy steel magnate, Andrew Carnegie once said, "Anything in life worth having is worth working for." In other words, if you think it's important, you'll work for it. You'll find a way to make it happen. Today's a great day to choose something meaningful. Something that would improve your quality of life. Choose it and get started!

It's tempting to take the easy path, but it's the path with the least reward. The decision is yours alone. You can give up, or you can push through.

What will you choose to work on today that might be difficult, but will truly make a difference in your life?

_____

_____

How does it feel to have made this decision and take the first step?

_____

_____

"The great gift of human beings is that we have the power of empathy, we can all sense a mysterious connection to each other."

- Meryl Streep

Day 140

The next time someone is rude and disrespectful toward you, pause just a moment, and instead of reacting, try imagining what could be going on in their life that influenced them to behave insensitively toward other people.

Creating clear boundaries, and not allowing people to treat you poorly, is important. But so is empathy and compassion. The cool thing about that is it has a dual effect, because when you show empathy it helps you as much as it helps the other person. Even if they don't respond in a positive way, you'll benefit just the same and not take their behavior personally.

Practice exercising empathy for difficult people by remembering a past experience when someone was rude to you.

What explanations can you come up with for their behavior that helps you feel empathy?

_____

_____

The next time a situation like this arises, what strategy can you use to curb your reaction and choose this approach instead?

_____

_____

"The miracle is this–the more we share, the more we have."

- Leonard Nimoy

Day 141

Sharing is a beautiful way to test positive. Even when going through a difficult time and you have little to offer, what you share still makes a huge difference. Generosity doesn't just benefit the person receiving, it also creates biochemical changes in the person doing the sharing. It creates a surge of serotonin, the good mood hormone and neurotransmitter that causes you to feel happy and content. Serotonin helps dial down your stress response and lessens the effect of stress hormones. Sharing is good for your health!

Being generous and sharing with others isn't just about money or material things. It's also your time, energy, prayers, food, listening, and more.

What will you share with those around you today?

_____

_____

How can you more graciously receive when someone wants to share with you?

_____

_____

"It matters not how strait the gate, How charged with punishments the scroll, I am the master of my fate, I am the captain of my soul."

- From the poem *Invictus*, by William Ernest Henley

Day 142

When you're in an oppressive environment of negativity, it's challenging to not get dragged down. Oftentimes, circumstances aren't within your control, but you are the master of your fate. You can control yourself and how you react to situations.

When things seem impossible, or too heavy to bear, remember that you've been through tough times before, and you made it through. When things looked dark and there seemed to be no way out, you found a way. No matter what you're facing today, you're going to make it again. You are the captain of your soul!

What circumstance are you currently experiencing that seem out of your control?

_____

_____

Instead of saying "I can't," ask yourself "How can I?" Write down your answers.

_____

_____

"We are all walking mirrors
with the power of reflecting
someone's light to them
when they've forgotten just
how bright they shine."

- Unknown

Day 143

Do you ever feel rotten about life, yourself, or things you've done or haven't done? Of course, we've all felt like that. And then someone comes to you for advice, or thanks you for something you did, and it changes everything about your day. It's a reminder of your own light and ability to change the day for someone else. Chances are, there'll be people who cross your path today who need you to mirror their light back to them and remind them of how bright they shine.

Instead of feeling bad about yourself, think of the accomplishments and traits that make you shine.

Who can you support today by mirroring their light back to them? Can you help them focus on their accomplishments and strengths?

"A bird sitting on a tree is never afraid of the branch breaking, because its trust is not on the branch but on its own wings."

- Charlie Wardle

Day 144

Everyone knows that worrying doesn't change anything, at least not for the better. What it does change is the amount of biochemical reactions in your body which causes cortisol to flood your system and potentially cause harm. All of that for nothing, because no amount of worrying will change the outcome of a situation.

Trust in yourself, and remember that you've made it through every single problem you've ever faced. Instead of worrying, warrior-up, you've got this!

What have you been worrying about that you can let go of today?

_____

_____

What action you can take toward solving the problem instead of worrying about it?

_____

_____

"Enjoy the little things in life because one day you'll look back and realize they were the big things."

- Kurt Vonnegut

Day 145

Today's a great day to test positive by focusing on what you have and expressing gratitude. When you direct all of your attention to what you don't have, it creates a negative state of mind and a scarcity mindset. However, when you cultivate a feeling of gratitude and abundance, you'll impact your health in a positive way, and attract more things to be thankful for!

What are you are most thankful for today?

_____

_____

How can you shift your focus away from what you don't have, and toward what you do have? Can you create a gratitude list?

_____

_____

"Never underestimate your light.
It may be your light that leads
others out of the darkness."

- Unknown

Day 146

Have you ever been annoyed by a phone call from someone that came at a busy time? Or maybe you were on your way home after a long day, and a stranger strikes up a conversation when all you really wanted was to get home and unwind. It's not unnatural to have those feelings, but what if you shifted your perspective a little?

It might be that those people were drawn to you because of your compassionate and caring energy—your light. That subtle change in viewpoint turns those interactions into opportunities. You never know how badly someone might need a kind word of support and encouragement, and a few minutes with you could make all the difference.

How can you be more attentive to the people who cross your path today?

_____

_____

Can you remember a time when the light of another lifted you up when you needed it the most? Describe how that felt and what happened.

_____

_____

"Don't wait until you've reached your goal to be proud of yourself. Be proud of every step you take toward reaching your goal."

- Unknown

Day 147

You receive a compliment from someone and respond with "Thank you, but…" Have you ever done that? They tell you that your outfit is beautiful and you say, "Thank you, but I've had this for so long." Or someone congratulates you on an achievement and you come back with, "Thanks, but it wasn't a big deal."

Too often we focus on mistakes, perceived flaws, or what we don't have, and fail to celebrate our wins. Self-improvement is great, but so is appreciating the person you've become and where you are in life. Test positive today by celebrating something about yourself!

What's your latest achievement, big or small, that you can pause and celebrate today?

_____

_____

How grateful are you that you've made it to where you are now?

_____

_____

"The real winners in life are the people who look at every situation with an expectation that they can make it work or make it better."

- Barbara Pletcher

Day 148

I remember coaching a client once who often used the words, "I can't." I asked him how he felt when he said those words. Naturally, they made him feel powerless to change anything. I wanted to help him flip the script, so I advised him to replace "I can't," with "How can I?"

That simple perspective shift changes everything. Limits turn into opportunities, and defeat transforms into victory. That's how the winners do it!

Evaluate when and why you say, "I can't." What's underneath?

_____

_____

How does the change to "How can I?" make you feel?

_____

_____

"A diamond is a chunk of coal that did well under pressure."

- Henry Kissinger

Day 149

Hey, I know how tough it can be. There are times when life seems like one challenge after another. After a while, you get tired of dealing with all the crap! But guess what, it's not crap. What you're experiencing is growth.

As unpleasant as it can be, personal growth can only happen when you're outside of what's comfortable. You grow only when you're challenged in some way, so when the pressure is on, just know you're becoming a diamond!

What personal growth might you experience from the difficulties you're facing right now?

_____

_____

How have past challenges helped you grow into the person you are today?

_____

_____

"Switch your mentality from
'I'm broken and helpless' to
'I'm growing and healing'
and watch how fast your
life changes for the better."

- Reyna Biddy

Day 150

Can you feel the difference between the two phrases from today's quote? One phrase places you firmly in the role of victim, while the other empowers you and puts you in a position of control.

It's crucial to remember that you hear every word you speak, and feel every thought you allow to remain in your mind. Test positive today by using your words and thoughts to empower, and speak to yourself (and about yourself) as you would to your best friend. You create your own beliefs, and you become what you believe.

What negative statements do you use that could be switched to empowering affirmations?

_____

_____

How can you help others do the same?

_____

_____

"May your choices reflect
your hopes, not your fears."

- Nelson Mandela

Day 151

How many choices have you made in life that were rooted in fear? You might have been afraid to make a decision, or afraid not to, but either way things probably didn't go as well as you'd hoped. That's what fear does, it attracts even more things to frighten you and you get stuck in an energetic boomerang that you actually created.

But here's the good news; you can just as easily make a positive boomerang by making choices born out of love for yourself and others. You get back what you put out into the Universe, so be sure to sow seeds of love, hope, peace, and confidence. Do this, and everything changes!

Reflect on some recent decisions. What emotion(s) were they rooted in?

_____

_____

How have fear-based decisions in your past affected your life? What about hope based decisions?

_____

_____

"Life is too short to be
serious all the time. So, if
you can't laugh at yourself,
call me, I'll laugh at you."

- Unknown

Day 152

Okay, just kidding. I wouldn't actually laugh at you, but I would laugh with you! Today's a great day to test positive by not taking anything too seriously—including yourself. Instead, release some of those good endorphins by laughing it up every chance you get. Goof off, act silly, call that friend who's constantly cracking you up, or go hang out with them for a while.

Look for a way to make things fun today!

If you're struggling with cutting loose today, who can you call to help you lighten up?

_____

_____

When was the last time you laughed uncontrollably, or had a low-pressure day of fun?

_____

_____

"Mindset is everything. The thoughts you have affect your energy and actions. When you change your thoughts, you change your life."

- Unknown

Day 153

Today's a great day to think about your thoughts, and test positive as a result! Research says that the average person has around 60,000 thoughts every day. Of those, 80% are negative, but that's not all. Out of those negative thoughts, 95% are on repeat. There's no way you can feel good or enjoy life with so many negative thoughts running through your mind.

You don't have to lie to yourself by pretending everything is okay all the time, but you can intentionally focus on gratitude, and direct your energy toward all the things in life that are going well for you. It will literally change your life!

What negative thoughts run on an endless loop in your mind?

_____

_____

What are some things you can focus on that fill you with gratitude?

_____

_____

"Forget not that the earth delights to feel your bare feet and the winds long to play with your hair."

- Khalil Gibran

Day 154

You're aware of the benefits of spending time outside. A vitamin D boost from the sun, fresh air, improved brain function, to name just a few. But there's another benefit to keep in mind, and one that many don't think about. Nature is also affected by you! You're made up of energy, and you're connected to every living thing inhabiting this planet. We often think about what we can get (or take) from nature, but what are you giving back? Remember, you don't just experience nature, you're a part of it!

When you go outside and appreciate the beauty of the world you live in, and express your heartfelt gratitude, you send beautiful and powerful energy to all living things. Test positive today by sending out good energy. Oh, and in case you're wondering—tree-hugging is a thing, so go for it!

What can you do outside today that will give you the opportunity to show some love to nature?

_____

_____

How will you act differently towards nature with this new perspective?

_____

_____

"Let not one person take away your sparkle today. Shine bright and have fabulous day!"

- Unknown

Day 155

I love to intentionally start my day, week or month, strong. I feel like it sets me up for success! Today, you can test positive by becoming bulletproof and unaffected by what's going on around you. Work on keeping your peace, your sparkle, and your light.

Don't give anyone or anything the power to influence you to be less than who you are. Even in the midst of a storm, a lighthouse continues to shine brightly!

What intention can you set today that will help you be in control of your thoughts and mood?

_____

_____

If something comes up to rattle you, what strategy can you use to regain control of your peace?

_____

_____

"The law of giving is very simple: If you want joy, give joy. If love is what you seek, offer love. If you crave material affluence, help others become prosperous."

- Deepak Chopra

Day 156

Today, testing positive is all about giving! Many of us give money to charities, and that's a good thing, but giving isn't just about money. In fact, there are many ways you can give to others. You could help them finish a project, run an errand, or support them as they make a tough decision.

Anything you can do to make someone's day easier, a little lighter, and less stressful, is an act of giving. The great thing about giving is that the more you do it, the richer your life will be!

Who do you know that could use a little of your charity in the form of time, assistance, or support?

_____

_____

"Out of suffering have emerged the strongest souls; the most massive characters are seared with scars."

- Khalil Gibran

Day 157

Today is a perfect time to acknowledge a fundamental truth: You have overcome every obstacle, scaled every mountain, and met every challenge you've ever encountered. How do I know that? YOU ARE STILL HERE!

You're a success, and a warrior! The scars you carry inside and out are evidence of your survival, so don't view them as weakness or failures. Stand tall and recognize them as badges of honor and symbols of your inner strength. I am so proud of you!

What skills have you used in the past to get through something that seemed insurmountable?

_____

_____

What scars of survival do you carry? Can you focus on some self-love towards those scars?

_____

_____

"The biggest lie we fall for is that it doesn't matter. Your opinion doesn't matter. Your choices don't matter. Your influence doesn't matter. Your existence doesn't matter. You don't matter…Don't fall for that evil lie. Don't forget that everything about you absolutely does matter."

- Richelle E. Goodrich

Day 158

Doesn't it feel wonderful to know you matter to someone, and to spend time doing things that are meaningful? It's often the so-called "small things" that have the biggest impact, and you may not be aware of how big a difference you make in the lives of others.

This can work in two different ways. You can both lift someone up or shatter them with a word, a look, or an action. Everything you do has the power to either heal or harm. Choose to be a healer!

What "small" act can you do today that'll have a big impact on someone else's quality of life?

_____

_____

What's "small" act can you do to impact **your** quality of life??

_____

_____

"You are afraid of
surrender because you
don't want to lose control.
But you never had control;
all you had was anxiety."

- Elizabeth Gilbert

Day 159

Testing positive today is about initiating a breakup. If you're wondering how that's a good thing, I'm talking about breakup with fear, worry, and anxiety about the future!

The only thing that changes when you worry about something is you, and those changes aren't good. Worrying causes stress, and stress releases hormones that can damage your body if they hang around for very long. Surrender to the knowledge that the only thing you can truly control is how you think and react. You'll make it through whatever you're facing. You always have, and you always will!

What are you worrying about that you're willing to let go of today?

_____

_____

Has worry negatively impacted your life? How can you change the way you deal with unsettling situations?

_____

_____

"Beneath every behavior there is a feeling. And beneath each feeling is a need. And when we meet that need, rather than focus on the behavior, we begin to deal with the cause, not the symptom."

- Ashleigh Warner

Day 160

The world can a pretty stressful place sometimes. Have you noticed how many people seem to be on the edge? They're easily angered, cranky, sad, or withdrawn. Often it seems there's no reason for their behavior.

Try testing positive today by looking past external behaviors and offering a little compassion and empathy. I don't mean you should give a free pass to someone who's being abusive or cruel. By all means set all necessary boundaries in those situations. What I am saying is that many people are struggling right now, and while they may seem cranky or sad for no reason, there's definitely a reason. Be the one who shows them love and light.

Who could use a little extra compassion and empathy today? And why?

_____

_____

How can you gently, and respectfully, set boundaries with people who are taking their emotions out on you?

_____

_____

"Be fearless in the pursuit of
what sets your soul on fire."

- Jennifer Lee

Day 161

When was the last time you felt your soul was on fire, and your heart was filled to the point of bursting with passion? If it's been a while, and you've been waiting for life to make you feel that way again, I've got some good news for you. You don't have to wait!

You have the power to create those experiences for yourself. What if you chose something that set your soul ablaze and made your heart pound with excitement? Well, you can!

What lights you up, but you haven't done in a while? Can you do that today?

_____

_____

How can you give this kind of experience to someone in your family, or a friend?

_____

_____

"Respect your body. Fuel your body. Challenge your body. Move your body, and most of all love your body."

- Booki Nova

Day 162

Test positive today with some physical self-care. Your body is the only place you'll ever live, so you must give it the care it deserves.

Garbage in equals garbage out, and that goes for both body and mind. Plus, a healthy body leads to a healthier mind. Another win/win situation! Show yourself a little love today. After all, you deserve it!

What act of physical self-care can you focus on today?

_____

_____

What types of self-care needs more frequent attention? (Exercise, relaxation, playtime, less sugar, etc.)

_____

_____

"Strength doesn't come from winning. Your struggles develop your strength. When you go through hardship and decide not to surrender, that is strength."

- Arnold Schwarzenegger

Day 163

I don't know about you, but I've been through some crap. I mean, some really tough situations! Those who know me best would describe me as a mentally tough person, but I didn't get that way by accident. I don't simply wake up that way every day, nor do I feel that way every moment of my life.

I practice mental toughness, much in the same way one exercises regularly. I get stronger through focused and intentional effort. And guess what—if I can do it, so can you!

What aspect of mental toughness can you focus on today?

_____

_____

What aspects of your life would be better or easier if you had more mental toughness?

_____

_____

"The energy we put out in the world is the energy we get back. So if you want more love in your life, set your intention to be more loving. If you seek kindness, focus your energy on empathy and compassion."

- Oprah Winfrey

Day 164

D o you know that whatever energy you send out into the world comes right back to you? Think of it as an energetic boomerang. When you embrace this truth, life becomes so much easier!

If you're unforgiving, angry, negative, or hurt most of the time, then you're going to experience more of those things in your life. But here's the great news; the opposite is equally true! The more love, passion, and kindness you put out there, the more you will experience them in your own life. How amazing is that?

Who have been angry with that you can send some love to today?

_____

_____

What would you like to experience more of in your life? Start putting that out there and watch it come back!!

_____

_____

"Treat everyone with kindness and respect. Not because they are nice, but because you are."

- Unknown

Day 165

L et's test positive today by choosing wisely how to react or respond to whatever we encounter throughout the day. Don't treat others the way they treat you. Instead, allow your treatment of others to be based on who you are, rather than on how you were treated.

When I'm tempted to react negatively toward someone who treated me with unkindness, I whisper this into my own ear, "You're better than that." It reminds me in an instant that the other person may be experiencing inner turmoil I know nothing about. That doesn't mean I excuse their behavior, but me lashing out at them will do nothing to improve either of our lives. Never allow anyone to negatively influence your behavior.

What phrase can you remind yourself with to stay in a mindset of kindness and empathy?

_____

_____

I love to use humor to defuse situations that could lead others to be unkind. What strategy can you use as a preventative measure?

_____

_____

"May the sun bring you new energy by day, may the moon softly restore you by night, may the rain wash away your worries, may the breeze blow new strength into your being, may you walk gently through the world and know it's beauty all the days of your life."

- Apache Blessing

Day 166

What a beautiful blessing this is, and an incredible way to approach every person you encounter. Remember the energetic boomerang we keep talking about? What you send out comes back to you!

So today, send this blessing to everyone you come in contact with, but make one small shift. Instead of the word "may" I would like to propose replacing it with the word "let."

Be intentional as you walk through this world, so you can really "...know it's beauty all the days of your life."

How will being intentional about sending out this blessing affect your day?

_____

_____

What makes it difficult to maintain this intention all day?

_____

_____

"Words. So powerful. They can crush a heart, or heal it. They can shame a soul, or liberate it. They can shatter dreams, or energize them. They can obstruct connection, or invite it. They can create defenses, or melt them. We have to use words wisely."

- Jeff Brown

Day 167

L et's test positive by paying attention to our words. It isn't only what you say, but also how you say it. Words can harm or heal in an instant, but once they're spoken they can't be taken back!

You may not have control over how people interpret what you say, but you can stack the deck in your favor by intentionally choosing kindness, compassion, empathy, love and healing. And sometimes, no words are needed to convey the same gifts.

How can you be more intentional with the words you use today, and the way you deliver them?

_____

_____

Who might you have offended (even unintentionally) by something you said, and could use an apology today?

_____

_____

"Do what scares you, your dreams are there waiting for you."

- Christina Perri

Day 168

How many times in your life can you look back on and say, "If I'd let my fear stop me, I wouldn't have experienced this?"

I can think of several in my own life. I wouldn't be a professional speaker if I'd let fear stop me. I wouldn't have had a radio show, and I wouldn't have had the opportunity to cohost the Women in Safety Breakfast Show if I'd let fear stop me.

Just go for it! Fear is a thought, but not necessarily a reality!

In what way might fear be holding you back from something you really want?

_____

_____

Who could help you deal with the fear, or what skills do you need in order to move past it?

_____

_____

"Speak from your mind and people will hear you with their mind. Speak from your heart and people will hear you with their heart."

- Marianne Williamson

Day 169

Someone once asked me what to say to his friend who was dying. He wanted to say the right thing. I gently advised him to ask his brain to be quiet, and let his heart speak.

Your heart always knows just what to say, and how to say it. Most importantly, others will feel the genuine sincerity of your words. Today is a perfect day to let your heart speak to those around you. It doesn't judge, it knows how to heal, and it always has the right words!

What is the difference between speaking from your mind versus speaking from your heart?

_____

_____

How do you think speaking from your heart with every person you talk to today will affect your day?

_____

_____

"The people who trigger us to feel negative emotion are messengers. They are messengers for the unhealed parts of our being."

- Teal Swan.

Day 170

Your triggers are your teachers, if you allow them to be. Take notice of who and what pushes your buttons and elicits negative emotions or reactions from you. The next time you have that experience, pause a moment to reflect, and ask yourself why you're feeling that way.

If appropriate in the moment, and it's a person who triggered you, let them know how you're feeling and see if you can work through it together. Chances are, they have no idea they even pushed your buttons, and some honest communication could be beneficial for both of you. If you feel you need some extra help, don't hesitate to ask a professional to assist you in working through any unresolved issues. If you remain stuck, those issues will live in your tissues and your health could be affected. You got this!

When was the last time something or someone triggered negative emotions in you?

_____

_____

Do you know why you were triggered, and how can you resolve the issue?

_____

_____

"You have to have help-
people with the same vision
as you and people you trust.
An amazing support system
is behind every success."

- Monica Potter

Day 171

Today's a great day to stay far away from people who don't support you in the pursuit of your dreams! Just like today's quote states, behind every success is an amazing support system that helped make it possible.

When you pursue a dream, and step outside of what others feel is comfortable, they may react with doubt and fear. Their reaction has nothing to do with you and your dream, but everything to do with their own fears. It's vital to limit your exposure to people like that because they'll drag you down. Keep your circle tight and hang out with people who believe in you!

Think of your last big success. Who helped you get there?

_____

_____

Who do you know who's pursing a dream, and how can you support them?

_____

_____

"You have no idea what people are dealing with in their personal lives so just be nice, it's that simple."

- Unknown

Day 172

Have you ever found out something new about a friend you've known for years? You thought you knew pretty much everything about them, then suddenly you discover they were raised in an abusive home or had a terrible car accident as a teenager. Even when you know someone well, it doesn't mean you know everything. This is even more true with coworkers or acquaintances. When you observe someone behaving irrationally, or being short-tempered, it's possible you're witnessing a trauma response to something that occurred in their life.

It's not an excuse for their behavior, but since you can't always know the life history of others, it's best if you default to a more compassionate disposition.

What are some things in the past that may have affected your behavior toward others at some point?

_____

_____

How would defaulting to a compassionate mindset affect your interactions with others?

_____

_____

"Sometimes you just need to talk about something–not to get sympathy or help, but just to kill its power by allowing the truth of things to hit the air."

- Karen Salmansohn

Day 173

Testing positive has never been about positivity over reality. It has never been about putting on rose-colored glasses and pretending everything is fine all the time. That's lying to yourself and will actually create more issues than it'll solve. Being positive means you acknowledge the reality of any given situation, even if it's bad, because you know it's temporary. You face it head-on and intentionally choose which thoughts receive your energy.

We all deal with fear, anger, sadness, grief, regret, shame, and so on. You don't have to pretend emotions are nonexistent. Talking about your feelings will help you release them and send them on their way!

When tough times show up, where do you direct your energy?

_____

_____

Who are the people in your life with whom you feel safe sharing your feelings?

_____

_____

"One's philosophy is not best expressed in words; it is expressed in the choices one makes … and the choices we make are ultimately our responsibility."

- Eleanor Roosevelt

Day 174

How would you like to be remembered? When you cross the minds of others, what characteristics would you love to be in the forefront? Do your answers align with your actions and life philosophy? If you want your behaviors to reflect love and compassion, you can't be filled with prejudice and harsh judgement at the same time.

Since your actions and life philosophy are inseparable, think about how you'd like to show up in the world and make adjustments to your thoughts and actions accordingly. You'll become what you think about the most, so focus on being driven by peace, love, and understanding. When that disposition aligns with your actions, you'll test positive in the lives of others every day!

How would you describe your life philosophy?

_____

_____

What adjustments could you make to your thinking patterns?

_____

_____

"No one has ever become poor by giving."

- Anne Frank

Day 175

Today is a beautiful day to focus on generosity! I'm talking about more than money too. You can also be generous with your time, help, kindness, compassion, and more. One who has the true spirit of giving never seeks a return on their generosity. But what's magical about this is, even when you don't give with expectation of return, you still receive. In fact, the more you give, the more you get in return. Isn't that amazing? It's a built-in bonus!

I mention energetic boomerangs often, and this is a prime example. Test positive today by instigating a boomerang of generosity!

Do you remember a time when you were on the receiving end of someone's generosity? How did it make you feel?

_____

_____

Who can you be generous toward today, and how can you demonstrate it through in your actions?

_____

_____

"Be the energy you
want to attract."

- Ralph Smart

Day 176

When things aren't going your way, it can be stressful and a real challenge to test positive. We sometimes get stuck thinking we can't change or control how we feel when things are difficult. While it's true that you can't always change circumstances, you can always change how you respond to them—and that's great news!

When you shift your perspective, you shift your energy at the same time. If something happens that prevents you from accomplishing something, instead of thinking it's over and saying "I can't do it," ask yourself, "How can I make this happen?" That subtle shift will change everything!

Think of a tough time you've experienced. How did you feel and respond?

_____

_____

How would things have been different if you had shifted your perspective and energy?

_____

_____

"Pooh, what's the bravest thing you've ever said?" asked Piglet.

"Help." said Pooh.

Day 177

I'm a recovering over-giver. Historically, receiving from others has been difficult for me, and asking for help when I needed it was terrifying, so I'd avoid it as much as possible.

Sound familiar? Needing help is often viewed as weakness, but the exact opposite is true. It takes a tremendous amount of strength to acknowledge you need help and be willing to ask for it. In fact, it's empowering! Plus, it's important to allow others to experience the amazing feeling of being a giver!

Do you struggle with receiving from others or asking for help?

Is there something you need help with today? Who can you ask?

"Be yourself. Accept yourself.
Value yourself. Forgive yourself.
Bless yourself. Express yourself.
Trust yourself. Love yourself.
Empower yourself."

- Lupytha Hermin

Day 178

Have you ever noticed that when you're feeling good about yourself, your day goes better? I talk about this a lot, but when you intentionally design your day to be a good one, rather than just wishing, the chances of you experiencing a great day will skyrocket.

Begin the day feeling good about yourself, because you deserve it!

What things do you love about yourself the most? Name them all!

_____

_____

Which part of today's quote do you feel drawn to today? Focus on that!

_____

_____

"The Universe responds to your frequency. It doesn't recognize your personal desires, wants, or needs. It only understands the frequency in which you are vibrating in…"

- Jake Woodard

Day 179

What you put out into the world comes back to you. It's easy to forget that the Universe isn't something "out there" that's separate from everything else. Everything is connected, including you, and what affects a part will affect the whole. Understand that the Universe has it's own language, in the form of frequency, vibration, and energy. Since you are part of the Universe, the same is true of you. Your thoughts, feelings, and emotions have energy, and the Universe is constantly responding to that energy.

Your state of mind, and the way you feel most of the time, will determine how you experience life. That doesn't mean you'll never have negative or heavy emotions, it just means feeling that way isn't the norm for you. Decide how you want to feel and what you would like to experience and focus your intention on thoughts that attract those things into your life!

How would you describe the way you feel most days?

_____

_____

Time to shift your perspective? Where can you focus your thoughts in order to raise your positive energy?

_____

_____

"If you're struggling and your people are just sitting there watching you struggle, they're not your people."

- Steve Maraboli

Day 180

I s it time to do some weeding in your relationship garden? It may sound harsh at first, but not everyone in your life needs to be in your life. If you take an honest look at your relationships, (friends or family) there'll be those who offer a helping hand when you're struggling, and those who always want help but never offer it.

The people who only take, and never give, will drain your energy. Sometimes, they may even be hurtful toward you. If you want to live a positive and joyful life filled with meaning and purpose, you must surround yourself with people who share a similar mindset. Those are your people!

Who are the people in your garden that might need to be weeded out?

_____

_____

How will surrounding yourself with caring and uplifting people affect your life? How can you be the same toward them?

_____

_____

"Respect your body when it's asking for a break. Respect your mind when it's seeking rest. Honor yourself when you need a moment for yourself."

- Unknown

Day 181

Consider the word, "no." It's a word that often gets a bad rap and is viewed as being negative, but that's not always the case. Sometimes, you have to say "**no**" in order to test positive! Your body will give you clues when it's ready for a break, and so will your mind. If you keep taking on more responsibilities, when your body is telling you to slow down, you're headed for trouble.

Listen when your body whispers what it needs and use the positive power of "no" whenever necessary. Give yourself time to recharge. After all, you can't pour from an empty cup!

Why do you struggle with saying "no" when you need a break?

_____

_____

How can you honor yourself today, and show respect to your body?

_____

_____

"People who uplift you are the best kind of people. You don't simply keep them. You have to treasure them."

- Dodinsky

Day 182

What a great day to test positive by thinking about the helpers and healers in your life! These are the people who make your heart sing and bring joy into everyday life. People like that are rare and magical, so be sure to let them know how much you treasure their presence in your life.

And while you're at it, look for ways to be that kind of person for someone else!

Who are the treasured and magical people in your life? Let them know!

_____

_____

How can you be that person for someone else today?

_____

_____

"Striving for excellence
motivates you; striving for
perfection is demoralizing."

- Harriet Braiker

Day 183

Today is the perfect day to choose effort and excellence over perfection! Please don't accept the lie that everything you do must be perfect, and if it isn't you're not good enough. That's garbage! Besides, who decides when something is perfect? Nobody, that's who.

Striving for excellence is inspiring and will keep you challenged and motivated. If you become stuck trying to "perfect" everything, you'll end up not doing anything at all. What's actually going on is fear of failure, or the opinions of others, is disguising itself as perfectionism. When you go for excellence and truly do your very best, it will always be good enough!

How has perfectionism stopped you from doing something important to you?

_____

_____

What dream can you reignite, and instead of perfection, strive for excellence?

_____

_____

"Very often, the little things we do for others are the exact things that keep their life from going into a spiral."

- Unknown

Day 184

Have you heard the expression "I'm praying for a miracle"? We've all said something similar at one time or another. Maybe it was "waiting for an angel" or even a "Christmas miracle," but what you're really saying during those times is that you're hoping for something or someone to change the trajectory of your life.

Just like you, there are people around you praying for a miracle, an angel or someone to help them. Your kindness, words, smile or small gesture could be exactly what they're waiting for. You could be their angel!

What kindness can you show today, and to whom?

_____

_____

Who has been the answer to one of your prayers? Can you let them know and express your gratitude?

_____

_____

"Difficulties of life are valuable opportunities for self-discovery."

- Lailah Gifty Akita

Day 185

Have you had a couple of tough years? Maybe more than a couple? It's safe to say that everyone experiences difficult times, sometimes resulting in suffering and loss. It can be painful, but if you're honest with yourself there's often something gained by facing intense challenges.

Testing positive means acknowledging the tough stuff, but also the gifts that come with difficult circumstances. For example, perhaps you've learned that the value of material things cannot compare to loving relationships. Perhaps you discovered you're stronger than you thought, or encountered opportunities that wouldn't have been possible otherwise. You can learn a lot about yourself by getting through hard times!

What gifts have you received from challenges you've faced in the last few years?

_____

_____

What's something you've learned about yourself during a difficult challenge in life?

_____

_____

"To be happy, you must create your own sunshine."

- C.E. Jerningham

Day 186

I t's easy to forget that love, joy, and happiness aren't random experiences. You have to create them, which isn't always easy, but it's always worth it! It's a great day to focus your thoughts on something, or someone, that puts a smile on your face and joy in your heart.

Here's the best part; when you have joy inside, it'll bring out the same in others, and just like an energetic boomerang, you'll attract even more joy!

How can you create some joy today?

_____

_____

What blocks you from creating more joy and happiness? How can you overcome these things?

_____

_____

"Dear past, thank you for
the lessons. Dear future,
I am ready."

- Unknown

Day 187

When you come to the end of a day, month, or year, take time to pause and reflect. If things didn't turn out like you wanted, it's okay to feel the emotions that go with it. The key is to not hang on to them indefinitely. If you hold on to bitterness, anger, or feelings of lack, you'll miss out on the wisdom that can help you create better tomorrows.

If you want to test positive, accept the lessons and beautiful gifts of wisdom that come with challenging circumstances. What you do today will create your tomorrows!

What is something from the past day, month or year, that you're incredibly grateful for?

_____

_____

How can you stack the deck on a future endeavor so things go the way you want?

_____

_____

"Talk to yourself like you would to someone you love."

- Brené Brown

Day 188

How many of us have beat ourselves up for not exercising, and underachieving during holiday seasons, summertime, or while on vacation? Too many, I bet. Does that negative self-talk motivate you to take better care of yourself or be more productive? Would you speak to your best friend the same way you speak to yourself? Instead of bullying yourself today, try testing positive with love and kindness.

Make this your mantra today:

"Today I love myself enough to do the very best I can—for me. I deserve to fill myself with beautiful thoughts, healthy food, and gently move my body that does so much for me. I'll protect myself from anyone, or anything, that doesn't contribute to my highest good, including my own thoughts."

How can you show up for yourself today as your greatest ally?

_____

_____

Write down the meanest thing you've ever said to yourself. Imagine saying that to someone you love and care about. Now, scribble it out and write down the opposite. Repeat this new mantra all day.

_____

_____

"If we did all the things we are capable of, we would literally astound ourselves."

- Thomas A. Edison

Day 189

So often, we look back on our past with criticism for what we did or didn't do. But what if you looked back on all the ways you showed up, grew up, and leveled up? That would be a real game-changer!

Look where you are now, and recognize how much courage and strength it took to get there. Look at how much you've learned. You are unstoppable!

When you look back over your past, what are you most proud of doing or accomplishing?

_____

_____

In what ways have you blown your own mind? How did you grow in ways you never expected?

_____

_____

"Unconditional love does not mean unconditional acceptance of bad behavior."

- Unknown

Day 190

Sometimes, testing positive is about how you can positively affect the lives of others, but today it's all about you. It's time to put yourself first! It's time to show up for yourself the same way you're always showing up for other people.

We talked about this a few months ago, but it's important so here's another reminder; you teach others how to treat you by what you allow and accept. So, stop putting up with crap behavior. If you allow someone to treat you badly, you are literally teaching them that you're okay with it. By the way, the same is true of how you treat yourself. You can't say you love yourself while also treating yourself poorly. You deserve better!

How can you show yourself some love today and put yourself first for a change?

_____

_____

Is there someone you've allowed to treat you badly? How can you set some boundaries with them?

_____

_____

"I've been hiding from exercise. I'm in the fitness protection program."

- Snoopy

Day 191

I f you've been a little overindulgent and lazy lately, it's time to get back on track! Today's the perfect time to prioritize moving your body. Don't get stuck in regret, or beat yourself up for letting things slip. Decide to do something about it instead! Take a walk, go for a bike ride, or whatever it takes to get moving and those endorphins pumping.

Want to feel even better? Spend part of your day outside. Nothing rejuvenates you like time in nature!

What kind of exercise can you do today that'll shake loose those negative feelings?

_____

_____

How can you motivate yourself from repeating a cycle of laziness or overindulgence?

_____

_____

"Be the type of person you
want to meet."

- Unknown

Day 192

L et's test positive by thinking about how we show up in the world. Think about it like this; are you the kind of person you'd enjoy meeting? When you view it like that, it's easier to see areas in which you could use a little work.

Take me for example, I really admire people who are patient, and I love meeting such people. I'm also aware I need to work on being more patient. By making a change within myself, I become more like the kind of people I admire!

What kind of people do you love to meet? What tweaks can you make to become more like them?

_____

_____

What are some traits you already possess that you also admire in others?

_____

_____

"Darkness cannot drive out darkness, only light can do that. Hate cannot drive out hate, only love can do that."

- Martin Luther King, Jr.

Day 193

Negative energy in the world can weigh heavy on you at times. Judgement, hatred, divisiveness, and anger seems to fill the air like a black cloud of toxic smoke. It might be tempting to give back what you're getting, but there's only one way out. You must respond with exactly the opposite.

How can you do that? By focusing and demonstrating peace, love, kindness, and compassion to everyone—especially those who think and believe differently than you. They're just as passionate about their beliefs as you are about yours. And it doesn't mean they're wrong, just different. That's why you have to meet them on the common ground of love, patience, and understanding. Let's test positive today by refusing to fuel divisiveness!

Do you know someone who has opposing views? How can you approach them differently today?

_____

_____

What strategies can you use to keep your peace in an often divided world?

_____

_____

"Serenity is not freedom
from the storm; but peace
amid the storm."

- S A Jefferson-Wright

Day 194

Carrying around worry, fear, or anger is a bit like carrying around a bag full of garbage. It's difficult, it's heavy, and it stinks! Testing positive today means finding a sense of peace, even if you're in the midst of a storm right now. You need to be able to reboot and recharge, but it takes intentional effort.

I like to use meditation and practice gratitude to help me dump the garbage and make room for the good stuff!

What strategies can you use to recharge and find some peace and serenity? What works for you?

_____

_____

What garbage are you carrying that's robbing you of peace?

_____

_____

"I stopped waiting for the light at the end of the tunnel and lit that bitch up myself."

- Unknown

Day 195

Acknowledging your own power will set you up to have an amazing day! There's no need to wait for all conditions to be perfect, because that's simply not going to happen. The only perfect time to stop or start doing something is now.

It's your life, no one else's, and if something's not working, you have the right, responsibility and privilege of changing it. Stop looking for the light and turn it on yourself!

What can you focus on today that will positively impact the quality of your life?

_____

_____

What excuses have you used to put off making these changes? Are you ready to make a change?

_____

_____

"You can't be bitter and expect your life to be sweet."

- Unknown

Day 196

You attract what you give out. Let's think about that for a moment. If you say you're broke or lacking money all the time, that reality will be reflected right back to you in an energetic boomerang. If you say you have no friends, you'll get that reflected back as well. If you say your life sucks, it will. You attract what you are, not necessarily what you want, and what you are is determined by the thoughts that dominate your mind.

I say this with love and respect, because I know it's easier said than done, especially in dark times. But you have to be intentional with your thoughts. I'm not saying to put on rose-colored glasses and pretend reality doesn't exist, but I am saying you can influence and create for yourself a new reality!

What would you like reflected back to you today? What should you focus on in order to make that happen?

_____

_____

How can you shift your focus from looking for the downside in every situation, to seeking out the good?

_____

_____

"Don't count the days,
make the days count."

- Muhammad Ali

Day 197

Instead of busying ourselves with counting the days, we need to make the days count. Since you can never know just how many days you have on Earth, each one should be treated as a precious gift!

Are your days meaningful? Do you feel good at the end of each day, knowing you did your best and accomplished what you could? Do you feel like you're making progress? If not, perhaps you're operating on auto pilot. Life is too short for that. Create the life you want, and make the days count!

What can you do to add more meaning to you days?

_____

_____

If you could change one aspect of your life, what would it be?

_____

_____

"If you don't design your own
life plan, chances are you'll
fall into someone else's plan.
And guess what they have
planned for you? Not much."

- Jim Rohn

Day 198

I once had a coaching client who described to me how he spent his non-work time. Hearing his answer, I asked one question, "Do you enjoy those things?" Crickets.

I asked him why was he spending time doing things he clearly did not enjoy. His response? Because someone said he should.

That's a perfect example of how you become powerless in your own life. If you wonder why you're not happy and peaceful, look first at whose life you're living. If it's not your own, you won't be happy, or healthy either for that matter. Take back your power and live life on your terms!

Have you given away your power? How can you take it back?

_____

_____

If you've allowed people, circumstances, or societal pressure, to take your power away, ask yourself why. How can you prevent it from happening again?

_____

_____

"One of the most sincere forms
of respect is actually listening
to what another has to say."

- Bryant H. McGill

Day 199

How does it feel when you're trying to talk to someone, and instead of paying attention, they're looking at their phone? Or they won't allow you to finish one sentence without interrupting, and then flip the conversation and make it all about them? If you're like me, you feel disrespected and a little ticked off!

Testing positive is about listening to someone with the intention of understanding, not simply waiting for your turn to talk. It's about not turning things around and making it all about you. One of the most important and powerful ingredients in communication is the ability to be a great listener. It's a skill worth developing!

How can you be more present in your interactions today?

_____

_____

Practice listening without responding until someone is finished speaking. What makes this hard? Try this in every conversation today!

_____

_____

"What if you just turn your
magic all the way the fuck on?"

- Hadiiya Barbel

Day 200

Have you ever met someone with charisma and wished you were more like them? They enter any room and everyone thinks, "Wow! They've got beautiful energy, and such a great vibe!"

While you're busy comparing and thinking you fall short, you're missing the obvious—you have your own magic! It's time for you to turn it all the way up! Then it'll be you lighting every room you enter.

What personal magic can you inject into your day? Your sense of humor, patience, or your way with customers? Bring it and rock it!

_____

_____

What quality in others do you admire and would like to work on building in yourself?

_____

_____

"You are **not** fat. You **have** fat. You also have fingernails, but you are not fingernails."

- Unknown

Day 201

What's your label? Stupid, broke, weak, unlovable, sick, unattractive, unqualified, depressed, lonely? As I wrote those words, I felt physically ill remembering the times I've used them to label myself at one time or another. It's painful to know I used to feel that way about myself, but no longer!

It's nearly impossible for you to grow, thrive, and live your full potential if you negatively label yourself. You'll become what you believe is true about yourself, so believe good things! Change your words, and you'll change your world. Break up with your negative labels, and create new ones that'll inspire you to become the best possible version of yourself.

What are some labels you've heard or said about yourself? Can you see how inaccurate they are?

_____

_____

Create a new, inspiring, and motivating, label that'll make you proud!

_____

_____

″The way you alchemize a soulless world into a sacred world is by treating everyone as if they are sacred until the sacred in them remembers″

- Sarah Durham Wilson

Day 202

As things constantly shift and change in the world, please remember that we're all different, yet we're equal. People will have different thoughts and opinions than you today, and that really needs to be okay. Remember that opinions are not facts, they're perspectives.

We're all here for a purpose and possess infinite value, so it's time to stop judging one another on our differences. Instead, let's pour our energy into discovering what we have in common. If we can start there, we'll change the world into a better place—for us and our children.

How can you steer your daily conversations so that they're focused more on the common ground you share with others, rather than differences?

_____

_____

How can you gently set some boundaries with people who want to sit in judgement of YOUR opinions?

_____

_____

"Don't sacrifice your peace
trying to point out someone's
true colors. Lack of character
always reveals itself in the end."

- Mandy Hale

Day 203

Have you ever been in a conversation with a person who was determined to shine a spotlight on someone else's bad character? It seems like there's always somebody talking trash about others like it was their job.

Don't, just don't.

Testing positive today is about not trash-talking other people, or even listening to someone else do it. Some people call it karma, but I call it an energetic boomerang. You get back what you give out, so be careful with what you're putting out there.

If someone comes to you with gossip about someone you know, how can you respond differently?

_____

_____

If complaining about others is a habit, how can you help yourself flip the script and be complimentary instead?

_____

_____

"Now every time I witness
a strong person, I want to know:
What dark did you conquer
in your story? Mountains do not
rise without earthquakes."

- Katherine MacKenett

Day 204

Think about a person you respect and admire; someone who has qualities you want to emulate in your own life. They might be strong, kind, generous, energetic, full of vitality, and successful. Whatever the admirable traits may be, they were likely forged in the fires of difficulty.

If you're facing a difficult time right now, rest assured that you're forging admirable traits of your own. When you make it through, you'll be stronger, wiser and better equipped to help others. Your light will shine even brighter!

What positive qualities do you possess that were the result of going through a hard time?

_____

_____

Write down the name of someone you admire, and their positive traits which you'd like to demonstrate in your life. Spend time with them, and ask how they came to live life the way they do.

_____

_____

Choose to focus your time,
energy and conversation around
people who inspire you, support
you and help you to grow you
into your happiest, strongest,
wisest self.

- Karen Salmansohn

Day 205

Test positive today by carefully choosing your environment. If you are a non-smoker, would you get into a vehicle with three chainsmokers and go on a road trip when it's -25C outside, and you can't open the windows? Absolutely not! And yet, we allow ourselves to become immersed in toxic negative energy. When that happens, is it any wonder why it's hard to be positive or grateful?

You can't "green smoothie" your way to good health if you're consistently exposed to negative energy. You have to clean up your environment, or find another one!

If you're in a toxic environment, what can you do today to clean it up? Note: a toxic environment can also be created in your mind.

_____

_____

What can you do to prevent being influenced by negative energy? It could be a circle of friends, workplace, family members, etc.

_____

_____

"The same red flags you ignore in the beginning will be the same reason it all ends."

- Unknown

Day 206

When you see red flags show up in a relationship, activity, or environment, ignoring them will only lead to more suffering. Red flags are clues that something is "off" and it's time to pay careful attention. Trust your intuition and tune in to what's going on before you find yourself on the edge of a cliff, metaphorically speaking, and being thrown off. Take notice and change whatever needs to be changed before things spiral out of control.

If you're already on the edge, testing positive means knowing that you'll not fall—you'll always fly. You have to trust your wings!

What red flags do you need to tune into today in a relationship, activity, or environment?

_____

_____

What stops you from tuning in to the red flags that come up in relationships? Can you see how this has led to your suffering?

_____

_____

"The greatest weapon against stress is our ability to choose one thought over another."

- William James

Day 207

Stress is the number one health epidemic in North America. This has been the case since long before the recent pandemic, but can you imagine how the suffering has been amplified? Please support those within your circle, and even those who aren't. You may not be able to take people's suffering from them, but you can let them know they're not alone.

Remember, if you see someone going through a similar situation as you, but they're handling it differently, it doesn't necessarily mean they're wrong. They're just dealing with it the best they know how, and need encouragement more than correction.

Don't take you own mental health for granted. Be intentional about managing stress, and nourish your body, mind, and soul every day!

What can you do to manage your stress effectively today?

_____

_____

What are some of the strategies you can use to prevent yourself from becoming stressed in the coming days and weeks?

_____

_____

"Yesterday I was clever, so
I wanted to change the
world. Today I am wise, so
I am changing myself."

- Rumi

Day 208

I t sure is easy to observe others and see how much they need to change, isn't it? I see this frequently with businesses when I go in to consult on things like culture and morale. It's common for people to blame others for their problems.

If you choose to view the world that way, you'll forever be at the mercy of other people's actions and decisions. I don't know about you, but I don't like being an emotional hostage to someone else. That's why I focus on myself, because I have control over what I do and think. Changing your self, changes your world!

What area of self-improvement can you work on today?

_____

_____

Why might you blame others for things not going well in your life? Can you see that these things are actually within your control?

_____

_____

"Whatever you are not changing, you are choosing."

- Laurie Buchanan, PhD

Day 209

D o you find yourself complaining about the same old things over and over? You make the same resolutions about the same things, but still nothing changes. Wishing for things to be different, and taking action to instigate change, are two very different things.

Even when you aren't making the needed changes that'll improve your quality of life, you're still taking action—you're choosing for things to remain the same!

If what you're doing isn't working, isn't it time to try something different?

What's not working in your life?

_____

_____

What are you prepared to do differently today in order to create something better?

_____

_____

"For my ally is the Force,
and a powerful ally it is."

- Yoda (Star Wars)

Day 210

D o you ever look at others and wonder how they can be so lucky? Things just seem to come easily to some people, but even when things don't go well, they seem content and confident. Do they have something that you don't have? Not at all, they've simply discovered how to tap into it.

We all have the force, a spark of divinity, or whatever you prefer to call it. The point is, you have everything you need to be happy and successful. When you accept this truth, you're well on your way to tapping into your own force!

Have you given up on your power to create and design the life of your dreams? Will you take the first step and you tap into your power by believing in yourself?

_____

_____

What small steps can you take to reclaim your power, to prove to yourself that you have what it takes to create success in whatever way you desire?

_____

_____

"The most common way people
people give up their power is by
thinking they don't have any."

- Alice Walker

Day 211

Testing positive means becoming aware of your words. How often do you utter the words, "I can't"? Try counting for a day or two and you might be surprised. Henry Ford once said, "Whether you think you can, or you think you can't, you're right." That quote perfectly expresses a fundamental truth; if you want to change your life, it all begins with your thinking. You're not powerless unless you believe yourself to be.

Try replacing "I can't," with "How can I"? It changes everything and puts the power back in your hands where it belongs, and where it always has been.

Where can you change your "I can't" to "How can I?" today?

_____

_____

Notice how often you default to negative thinking. What strategies can you use increase your awareness of this, and redirect your energy to more empowering thoughts?

_____

_____

"Love isn't a state of perfect caring. It is an active noun like struggle. To love someone is to strive to accept that person exactly the way he or she is, right here and now."

- Fred Rogers

Day 212

Why do we sometimes wish other people would change? It's usually because they're not the same as us. When you live with constant disappointment in others, it hurts you as much, if not more, than it does them. In fact, you'll create injury to your nervous system, no to mention your mental health. The key is letting go of your expectations of others, and accept their differences.

That doesn't mean you should accept or normalize bad behavior, but it does mean acknowledging that everyone has their own views and perspective. Just because they're different than yours doesn't mean they're wrong. Embracing this truth will strengthen your relationships, and improve your sense of well-being!

If someone rubs you the wrong way today, ask yourself why it bothered you. Why are you letting someone get under your skin and create a stress response in your body? Remember your triggers are your teachers.

_____

_____

What mental tweaks can you make so that other people's behavior doesn't affect you?

_____

_____

"We've been infected with this idea that love is an emotion only felt between two people. But love is universal. An energy. A contagious force. A gift. To offer money to a homeless man is to love. To save a worm from the sun is to love. To smile at a stranger is love. To be grateful, to be hopeful, to be brave, to be forgiving, to be proud, is to love."

- a.r.lucas

Day 213

Today's quote offers us a beautiful definition of love. Even the smallest of gestures can make a huge difference. Testing positive today is about showing love; smiling at a stranger, holding a door, commending an employee to their manager, or helping a child with their homework.

The beautiful thing about showing up in the world this way is the energetic boomerang you'll create. You'll get back whatever you put out!

What can you do to show a little love today?

_____

_____

How will you respond if your gesture isn't appreciated or valued?

_____

_____

"Sometimes, the strength within you is not a big fiery flame for all to see, it is just a tiny spark that whispers softly 'You got this, keep going.'"

- Unknown

Day 214

Recently, I spoke with a friend who was upset about a few things she was struggling to accomplish. During our talk she said, "I don't know how you got through the last few years. You are amazing!"

The truth is, I'm not any more amazing than anyone else. What is amazing are the strategies for success I use to keep myself going. Testing positive every day is one such strategy. Being intentional about my attitude is another. I bet there are techniques you use that make you amazing too!

What strategies can you use, or are already using, to help you be intentional, positive and successful?

_____

_____

Describe how you're intentional about designing life, instead of being a passive recipient. Create, don't wait!

_____

_____

"The thoughts we choose to think are the tools we use to paint the canvas of our lives."

- Louise L. Hay

Day 215

It's pretty easy to control your actions. If someone cuts you off in traffic, the thought might cross your mind to bump into the back of their car at the next stoplight. Naturally, you don't. You control the action easily because of the consequences, but can you control even the **thought** of doing it? Your thoughts are much harder to control than your actions, and they can cause multiple negative physiological reactions in your body which can harm your health. Let's put this into perspective to see just how much damage you could be causing biochemically.

According to the National Science Foundation, the average person has about 12,000 to 60,000 thoughts per day. Of those 80% are negative and 95% are repetitive.

How's your painting coming along? Does the canvas of your life reflect the way you want to live?

How can you create more positive thoughts and actions today?

_____

_____

What negative thoughts are on replay in your mind? Awareness is the first step to changing!

_____

_____

"You can't litter negativity everywhere and then wonder why you've got a trashy life."

- Unknown

Day 216

You've read about the energetic boomerang often in these pages. It's a real thing! If you complain about your life, finances, children, spouse, friends or family, the universe will deliver more things for you to complain about. You can't have a happy life if you see negativity in everything.

Things will still be tough sometimes, and I'm not suggesting you pretend everything is great when they're not. I'm suggesting that you try to focus more energy on the good things than you do on the bad things. That way you can attract more of the good stuff!

What are some good things in your life for which you're grateful?

_____

_____

How can you flip the script by not complaining about the bad, and start explaining why your life is so good?

_____

_____

"I don't take anything personally. I am a secondary character in other people's stories. I know that whatever people say about me is just a projection of their image of me. It has nothing to do with me."

- Miguel Ruiz

Day 217

You can test positive today by being unoffendable. I know it's challenging to not feel hurt or angered when someone lashes out at you, but it helps to understand that whatever the other person has going on, it has little to do with you.

Someone once said, "Hurt people, hurt people," and it's true. When a person carries inside of themselves some kind of trauma or emotional wound, it colors their view of the world and others. Most things they do and say will be from that place of pain, and it'll continue to negatively affect their life until it's dealt with and healed. You never have to tolerate or excuse bad behavior, but a little compassion and understanding goes a long way!

Do you remember a time when someone lashed out at you for no reason? Could they be hurting inside?

_____

_____

How will understanding that people's words and actions often have nothing to do with you change the way you react?

_____

_____

"So, what if, instead of thinking about solving your whole life, you just think about adding additional good things. One at a time. Just let your pile of good things grow."

- Rainbow Rowell

Day 218

If you think of everything in your life you'd like changed it can be overwhelming. That's why I love the idea of adding just a few good things here and there, instead of trying to transform everything all at once. It's how I approach things when introducing healthier eating to my coaching clients. Rather than asking them to stop eating all the things they shouldn't, I simply ask them to add more vegetables and fruit to what they'd normally eat. Over time, they include more healthy foods into their lifestyle, and less of the bad stuff.

When you add more good things into your life, you naturally begin letting go of things that no longer serve you. Nowhere is it written in stone that change always has to be hard!

In what areas of your life do you want to experience change?

_____

_____

What are a few good things you can begin adding to your life that will help bring about your desired changes?

_____

_____

"If you're not open to constructive criticism, then you're not open to truly growing as a person."

- Unknown

Day 219

Few people will criticize you more than yourself. I bet you're nodding your head right now. We are so quick to criticize ourselves and pinpoint all the ways we seemingly fall short, which wouldn't be a huge issue if it was constructive, but it usually isn't. Beating yourself up about every perceived shortcoming will never result in a positive outcome.

Don't get me wrong, it's great to look at what you're doing and do an honest assessment. That's how you experience personal growth and positive change. It's also valuable to remain open to feedback from other people, as long as it's constructive and not destructive. The key is knowing the difference!

How would you describe your style of self-criticism? Destructive or constructive? If it's destructive, how can you change that?

_____

_____

When was the last time another person critiqued something you said or did? Was it constructive feedback, or destructive?

_____

_____

"Sometimes the bad things
that happen in our lives put
us directly on the path to the
most wonderful things that
will ever happen to us"

- Nicole Reed

Day 220

If you've been to one of my presentations about stress, you've heard me say, "If you're going through a good time in your life, enjoy it because it'll come to an end. If you happen to be going through a tough time right now, hang in there because it'll also come to an end."

That's how life works. It's a constant ebb and flow of positive and negative experiences. How you get through the hard times is based primarily on your perspective toward life. Stay curious and open to change, and you'll see that challenging circumstances often lead to amazing opportunities and experiences!

Have you noticed this ebb and flow in your own life?

_____

_____

How can you shift your perspective during difficult times so that you remain open to possibilities?

_____

_____

"Work hard at relaxing and feeling good. It's one of the most productive things you can do."

- Unknown

Day 221

Hustle and grind. It's a lifestyle that has taken center stage in most western societies. It's celebrated and often touted as the only way to success. I find it mind-boggling that so many have come to accept burnout and an unhealthy lifestyle as the price one must pay for achievement. There are times when intense effort is needed, and hard work will always be part of any success story, but you can achieve your goals and dreams without sacrificing your physical and mental health.

While it's easy in western cultures to be intentional in our work, it isn't so easy to be as intentional with our rest. You can change this through practice though, and you'll be so glad you did. Everything in your life will improve when you take time to relax and recharge!

When do you find it difficult to "switch off" and enjoy downtime?

_____

_____

How can you bring more time for relaxation and recharging into your life? Can you try scheduling it?

_____

_____

"Your calm mind is the
ultimate weapon against
your challenges. So relax."

- Bryant McGill

Day 222

Calm mind? Are you serious right now? With everything that's going on in the world? If any of those questions crossed your mind when you read today's quote, I feel you. It seems almost counterintuitive doesn't it? But here's the thing, if your mind is in chaos, then so is your body. It's a nasty loop that self-perpetuates if you can't find calm in the midst of the storm. When your body is subjected to continuous stress, it'll give you warnings via physical symptoms. If those warnings are ignored, you're putting your heath in serious jeopardy.

It's not easy to be calm when surrounded by chaos, and it's okay to ask for help if you need it. Meditation, exercise, music, yoga, therapy—find something that works for you!

When your mind and body are in a constant state of stress, what are the clues (symptoms) telling you to find your calm?

_____

_____

What techniques or practices can you use to help you calm your mind and body?

_____

_____

"Be the safe space for your people. Let them bring bad news, the hard truth, and the heavy grief. Love them just as they are."

- Lauren Fortenberry

Day 223

Hey, are you that person? You know, the person who says, "Oh Yeah? I have bigger problems than you!" Maybe you should use different words. When someone comes to you with an issue, don't try to one up them or make it about you. Today is a great day to listen with the intention of understanding, and do so without any judgment. It's easy to view other people's problems and judge them to be smaller than yours. But it isn't about how you view their problems, it's how **they** see them, and to them they may be a huge!.

Practice empathic listening. Not in order to respond, but so you can better understand. Avoid interrupting others when they're sharing their concerns with you. Try using non-verbal communication to encourage them to continue speaking. Nodding your head, leaning in, and making eye contact, are far more effective techniques. The kindest thing to say is, "How can I help you? What do you need from me?"

Can you remember a time when someone gave you space to share your heart? How did that make you feel?

_____

_____

Who in your life that needs the same from you?

_____

_____

"Real growth is when you start checking and correcting yourself. Instead of blaming others, you take your power back by being responsible for your life."

- Unknown

Day 224

Test positive by taking back your power today! We tend to give others the power to affect our mood, health, actions, habits, and even choices. For example, "I can't lose weight because my partner keeps buying junk food." Is it **really** true that you can't? No. It's a lie we tell ourselves that makes us a victim of other people's choices.

By choosing to be responsible for your own actions and decisions, you put the power back where it belongs—in your hands!

Where can you take your power back today?

_____

_____

Why have you given others the power to make decisions for you? What's really behind it? Fear, insecurity, indecision?

_____

_____

"I don't fix problems, I fix my thinking. Then problems fix themselves.

- Louise Hay

Day 225

When you change your perspective, everything changes. Isn't that so true? Yet, we often forget this when in the middle of a challenge. Life is 10% what happens to us, and 90% how we react.

Test positive today by looking at things differently. I'm not saying you should put on rose-colored glasses and pretend all is well, you should acknowledge when things are tough, but if you dwell on it your issues will live in your tissues!

What issue are you dealing with in your life right now that could use a perspective shift?

_____

_____

What keeps you stuck with a negative perspective? What changes in thinking can you implement to turn it around?

_____

_____

"The real question is not whether life exists after death. The real question is whether you are alive before death."

- Osho

Day 226

Today is a great day to take stock of your life. I once asked a coaching client to share with me what made them light up and filled their heart with meaning. Silence. I watched them struggle as they searched for an answer.

Please, stop waiting to live! Stop just existing!

That which makes life worth living, the things that make your heart happy and fills you with joy won't suddenly fall from the sky. You must create, pursue, and take consistent action toward them. Be intentional every day, because tomorrow is not promised!

What can you do today that will fill your heart with joy, and light up your soul?

_____

_____

What prevents you from taking daily steps and creating your own happiness?

_____

_____

"All that I seek is already within me."

- Louise Hay

Day 227

R emember who you really are! It's time to celebrate how far you've come, how much you've grown, and acknowledge your strength.

We've been taught from a young age not to toot our own horn, but today you have permission, so toot away! Focus on the things that you're good at. Remember everything you need to get through the next hurdle in life, is already within you. How can I know that? Because who you are inside has gotten you through every hurdle you've ever faced. They are all in the past.

Go and be the rockstar that you are!

What are you good at that you can celebrate today?

_____

_____

What skills and strategies have you used to overcome obstacles and difficult challenges?

_____

_____

"Calmness is a human superpower. The ability to not overreact or take things personally keeps your mind clear and your heart at peace."

- Marc and Angel Chernoff

Day 228

Have you ever started your day in a great mood, and then someone came along and did something to ruin it? Of course, we've all experienced that at one time or another.

The thing is, if you allow someone to ruin your day it impacts your health (neurologically, biochemically, and spiritually) in a negative way, not theirs!

Stop giving anyone or anything the power to influence your health. Your superpower is remaining calm, and in control, as you create your own well-being.

How can you insulate yourself from the moods and energy of other people today?

_____

_____

What strategy can you use to regain your calm and create your own well-being if someone starts getting to you?

_____

_____

"The goal is progress, not perfection."

- Kathy Freston

Day 229

Practice makes perfect. Did you grow up hearing those words as often as I did? It almost seems reasonable, but it's a lie that's trying to convince us that we must be perfect at whatever we do, or we're not good enough. Inevitably, this leads to an unwillingness to try anything new. Fear of failure takes over and keeps us stuck.

Are you ready to test positive today? Choose effort and excellence over perfection, and remember your goal is progress!

Has fear of imperfection made you hesitant to try something new? Are you willing to choose effort and excellence and try anyway?

_____

_____

What strategy can you use to let go of the perfection lie? What evidence can you find that you are more than good enough?

_____

_____

"If you don't like something, change it. If you can't change it, change your attitude."

- Maya Angelou

Day 230

Isn't it stressful when things aren't going your way? You may feel like you're stuck and unable to change the circumstances. But let me tell you a little secret; there's always something you can change, even if it's only yourself!

It's true, and it works 100% of the time. Shifting your perspective, changing your attitude about things, will change your life. Every. Single. Time.

Describe a situation you're convinced you're unable to change. How can you shift your perspective on it?

_____

_____

What strategies can you use to prevent becoming stressed out and feeling like you have no control?

_____

_____

"You are stronger than your challenges and your challenges are making you stronger."

- Karen Salmansohn

Day 231

Today, you can test positive by celebrating the strong people in your life. While you're at it, celebrate yourself too! You may forget, during stressful times, that you're fierce, brave, and full of fire. I encourage you to take a moment to recognize and reconnect with your inner strength, and with the strong people in your life.

I want you to know that you're amazing!

What have you accomplished recently that makes you proud? Have there been tough times you worked through?

_____

_____

Who has inspired you? Who has been a strong and consistent ally in difficult times?

_____

_____

"Self-care is giving the world
the best of you, instead of
what's left of you."

- Katie Reed

Day 232

Today, test positive with some self-love. You can get started by choosing to not engage in anything, or with anyone, which harms you in any way. Create healthy boundaries, fuel your body with fresh, heathy foods, and soothe your mind by focusing only on things that are within your control.

I know you want to help people any way possible, and you work hard to be there for others, but you can only give what you already have. When you practice self-care, you strengthen yourself and will have more to offer. It isn't selfish to care for yourself!

Have you been neglecting yourself? How has that affected you?

_____

_____

Name a few ways that you'll practice some self-love today.

_____

_____

"When you try to control
everything, you enjoy
nothing. Sometimes you just
need to relax, breathe, let go
and live in the moment."

- Unknown

Day 233

If you experience a lot of worry or anxiety, you might be living too much in the past or the future. The best way to avoid this is to direct your attention to the present moment. The past is over and there's nothing you can do to change it, and your control over the future is limited. When you live in any other place besides the present, you create an anxious space to live, and miss everything that's happening right now!

Instead of being caught up in the past, or worrying about what may happen in the future, take time to appreciate where you are, what you're doing, and who you're spending time with. Live in the present moment and savor every second!

Are you caught up in the past, or worry about the future? Why?

_____

_____

Try using gratitude to bring you back into the present. What are you grateful for in this moment?

_____

_____

"You can't keep getting
mad at people for sucking
the life out of you, if you
keep giving them the straw."

- Unknown

Day 234

Energy vampires. They're everywhere. People who drain all of your positive energy and leave you mentally exhausted. People like that can wreak havoc on your life if you don't have strategies to deal with them. The good news is that you are in control of who you associate with. If you're regularly exposed to a super-negative person, it's time to stop spending time with them.

Some individuals seem to wake up and choose unhappiness every day, and to feed their hunger for negativity they'll work tirelessly to bring others down to their level. However, they can't suck the life out of you if you take away the straw!

Do you have energy vampires in your life? How do they make you feel?

_____

_____

What steps can you take to limit your exposure to super-negative people?

_____

_____

"Today I am making the decision to let go of the things that don't make me happy. I am letting go, happily."

- Unknown

Day 235

D o you have any relationships or responsibilities in your life that add zero value? Are you playing roles that rob you of joy and peace? If so, how can you be happy living under those circumstances?

Sometimes, you may find yourself in situations and not even know how it all began. That's okay, the important thing is being aware of things in your life that are hindering your joy. Once you clearly see the obstacles, you can figure out how to get around them and move on. Happily let them go!

Who or what, do you believe, are roadblocks to your happiness?

_____

_____

What actions can you take to change things?

_____

_____

"You," he said, "are a
terribly real thing in a
terribly false world, and
that, I believe, is why you
are in so much pain."

- Emilie Autumn

Day 236

E nergy. You put out a certain kind of energy, and people can feel it. The reverse is also true. The people in your life project energy too, and you're affected by it. This is why it's crucial for your well-being to surround yourself with the right people.

When a group of individuals come together in a harmonious way, everyone will reap the benefits. It's magical how peace, happiness, and a sense of purpose increases when you intentionally create a thriving environment!

Think of the people you associate with on a regular basis. In what ways does their energy affect you?

_____

_____

What actions can you take to create a more thriving environment?

_____

_____

"It never hurts to keep looking for sunshine."

- Eeyore

Day 237

There are tough days, and then there are days that make you wonder if you'll survive. I've been there a few times. I bet you have too. What helps me get through difficult times is finding just one thing for which I can be grateful. I won't pretend it's always easy, but good things happen when you bring gratitude into the picture.

Besides shifting your perspective and improving your mindset, it also changes you biochemically. It boosts your mood, energy, and helps you attract more things into your life that'll make you feel even more grateful. So, keep looking for the sunshine!

How do you get through tough days?

_____

_____

What makes you feel gratitude? Focus on those things today!

_____

_____

"If it's important you'll find a way. If it's not, you'll find an excuse."

- Ryan Blair

Day 238

A re you in your own way? Are there things you've wanted to accomplish, but there are always a dozen reasons why they've never happened? There's going to be challenges and obstacles no matter what goals you're pursuing, but if you continue blaming external circumstances your situation will never change.

Blaming circumstances, or other people, makes it more palatable to your ego, but when you accept full responsibility for your life, the changes come much quicker. You have what it takes to mold your life in whatever way you wish! Isn't it time to get out of your own way and make your dreams come true?

What dreams have you placed on hold due to external factors?

_____

_____

How can you get out of your own way? Can you start today?

_____

_____

"Staying quiet in order
to avoid external conflict
simply transmutes the
conflict inward. For the
sake of 'keeping the peace'
we create a battle inside."

- Unknown

Day 239

Being a peacemaker is a good thing, but it doesn't mean you shouldn't speak up in every situation. Suppressing how you feel doesn't mean your emotions simply disappear. They're still there, simmering below the surface, and waiting to boil over.

You know where all that energy goes? Into your body! Your cells, tissues, and organs become the battleground as all those pent-up emotions wreak havoc on your body, not to mention your mental health. You can speak your truth with love and respect!

Do you typically stay quite in order to keep the peace? How does that make you feel?

_____

_____

What feelings have you bottled up recently? How can you release them in a positive way?

_____

_____

"Contrary to popular opinion, quitting is for winners. Knowing when to quit, change direction, leave a toxic situation, demand more from life, give up on something that wasn't working and move on, is a very important skill that people who win at life all seem to have."

- Steven Bartlett

Day 240

I s it time for you to quit? Funny isn't it, how that phrase carries with it a negative feeling? We're often programmed to believe that quitting is always a bad thing, but that's not the case at all. While giving up can certainly have dire consequences, continuing to do something that's causing stress and draining your emotional battery can have horrible consequences as well. Sometimes, testing positive mean quitting!

Are you in a work or living situation that isn't working no matter how hard or long you try? It's important to be honest with yourself. Are things not going well because you're not doing all you can to help them improve, or are you spinning your wheels because it's time to remove yourself from the situation? Only you can answer that question, but if it's truly time to quit, then do so without guilt. Whatever's keeping you stuck is what you're trading for your well-being!

What situation would you like to quit, but feel guilty for doing so?

_____

_____

What else could you try or is it time to quit?

_____

_____

"The hurrier I go,
the behinder I get."

- Unknown

Day 241

Do you feel like you're constantly running from one thing to the next? If the feeling of being overwhelmed is a normal part of your day, it's time to take a step back and analyze what's really going on. It's possible you're addicted to being busy.

Being busy is habit-forming. Western culture prides itself on being in a perpetual state of busyness, but it's an addiction in dire need of a cure. You can test positive by kicking the habit! Look closely and pinpoint what's being fulfilled inside of you by being busy. It may be that you're actually avoiding something by distracting yourself with multiple tasks. Try setting just one goal at a time. Accomplish it before moving on to the next, and schedule in time to recharge in between!

Are you addicted to being busy? How does it manifest?

_____

_____

Is there something you're avoiding by being busy? Name other ways you can kick the busyness habit!

_____

_____

"One doesn't have to operate with great malice to do great harm. The absence of empathy and understanding are sufficient."

- Charles M. Blow

Day 242

Some of greatest pain I've experienced in relationships was due to lack of empathy and understanding. At work, or home, it doesn't matter. Sometimes, hurt people aren't looking for a solution to their problems as much as they're seeking to be seen, felt, and understood.

Humans are designed to naturally behave in this way. That's why you usually laugh when you see others laughing, or wince when someone else touches a hot stove. The trouble is that society often programs you to hide your feelings, which is seldom healthy. You might be good at showing empathy already, but you can get even better by seeing things from the viewpoint of others. Put yourself in their shoes, then test positive by giving them the gift of being seen and understood!

How do you feel when someone understands and empathizes with what you're going through?

_____

_____

Who needs your empathy and support right now?

_____

_____

"The best project you'll
ever work on is you."

- Sonny Franco

Day 243

I t's easy to get caught up in thinking of how other people could improve, but you can test positive today by focusing on you! I remind myself often that the best way for me to serve and help others is to become the best possible version of myself.

You don't have to make quantum leaps every day either. It's about making small positive changes and being consistent. It could mean facing a fear, sticking to a routine, or simply sharing your beautiful smile with others. Don't look outside of yourself for the magic to change your life. It's inside of you!

Focus and identify areas in which you'd love to improve.

_____

_____

What are a few small, positive changes you can begin to implement today?

_____

_____

"God gave us mouths that close and ears that don't. That should tell us something."

- Eugene O'Neill

Day 244

L istening is both a skill and an art. Many people listen only with the intent of responding, but what about listening with the intention of understanding instead? Changes everything, doesn't it?

Relationships thrive when active listening takes center stage. Rollo May once said, "There is no greater gift that one human being can give to another than that of understanding." Today is a great day to give this gift to those around you!

What does it feel like when someone truly listens to you?

_____

_____

Which relationships in your life can be improved with more active listening?

_____

_____

"Survival mode is supposed
to be a phase that helps
save your life. It is not meant
to be how you live."

- Michele Rosenthal

Day 245

Read today's quote once more, and then give it some serious thought. The stress response is supposed to be a temporary state, not a lifestyle. If it becomes a way of life, the risks to your healthy rise exponentially.

Instead of shrugging your shoulders and saying, "It is what it is," find a way out! Develop healthy coping skills, eat real food, get enough sleep, create personal boundaries, and ask for professional help if necessary. It's time to move way beyond surviving, and into thriving!

What's keeping you in survival mode?

_____

_____

What steps do you need to take to begin thriving, rather than merely surviving?

_____

_____

"You can't heal what
you can't feel."

- John Bradshaw

Day 246

I've said it before, and I'm going to say it again. Whenever you feel strong, negative emotions, whatever triggered them is a clue to something within you that needs healing. Your triggers are your teachers. It's easy to ignore them, blame other people or circumstances, but the way out is turning your attention inward and revealing what needs to be healed.

The scenario will repeat itself again and again, until you deal with the source. Give yourself permission to feel your emotions without guilt or judgment. Allow them to lead you to what triggered them in the first place. Once you feel and understand what lies beneath, your healing begins!

Are you experiencing strong, negative emotions? List them.

_____

_____

Now dig deeper. Look inside and uncover what is triggering those emotions. What lies beneath the trigger?

_____

_____

"There are two places
you need to go to often.
1. The place that heals you.
2. The place that inspires you."

- Unknown

Day 247

I'm testing positive today, are you in? You can begin by making time for yourself! Sounds simple enough, but I know firsthand how challenging it can be. "I don't have time," often becomes a daily mantra while your physical and mental health suffers.

Everyone has something that heals and inspires them. It could be meditating in nature, a morning run, or a quiet evening at home. When you're too busy to take time for yourself, that's a clue that you need to run to whatever it is that rejuvenates your heart and soul. Imagine the peace, health, and happiness you'll experience!

What are you too busy with lately, to take time for yourself?

_____

_____

What is it that heals and inspires you? Please make time for that in your life!

_____

_____

"Don't let people pull you
into their storm. Pull
them into your peace."

- Kimberly Jones

Day 248

You choose your perspective and reactions. Every day. You could blame other people for lack of peace, but inside you know it's up to you. It's tough sometimes, especially with how some people behave, but keep in mind that they're choosing their reactions too. Which means they're in need of peace, just like you.

Rather than allowing them to pull you into their storm, let your compassionate heart draw them into your peaceful energy! You can protect your peace from the ones who refuse to change by creating boundaries and sticking to them.

What perspective will you choose today? How will that affect your interactions with others?

_____

_____

How can you create healthy boundaries to protect your peace?

_____

_____

"Stop looking for things
you know will upset you."

- Unknown

Day 249

id you know you can become addicted to stress and chaos? Hormones and biochemical compounds produced by your body when it's in fight-or-flight mode are addictive, and so much so that you can subconsciously create unnecessary drama just to feed the need. Escalating the production of these stress hormones can be a dangerous game with serious health risks.

There's good news though. You can kick the habit by consciously choosing to shift your focus onto things that create happiness and peace in your heart. Don't be fooled by the simplicity because this will transform your life!

Examine your life. How might you be creating chaos and stress in your life?

_____

_____

What can you focus on that brings you happiness and peace?

_____

_____

"Life is so much
more than what we
see on the surface."

- Gail Lynne Goodwin.

Day 250

Things aren't always as they seem. If you judge others based solely on what you see or hear, you might misinterpret the situation altogether. Have you ever acted brave, but inside you were terrified? Have you ever worn a smile on your face, even though you were hurting on the inside? Other people do that too.

It's a great day to test positive by being mindful of this, and that what you're seeing on the surface may be misleading. At work, or home, be aware that people often disguise their distress. They may appear confident on the outside, but feel the opposite on the inside. Conversely, they may be bitter and lash out at others because of the hidden pain they're experiencing within. Lead with kindness and compassion in every situation!

Have you ever disguised your pain? How well did it work for you?

_____

_____

Do you know someone who might be hiding their pain or fear? How can you show them kindness and compassion today?

_____

_____

Four things you can't recover:

The stone after it's thrown.
The word after it's said.
The occasion after it's missed.
The time after it's gone.

- Deanna Wadsworth

Day 251

Regret is a leading cause of depression. Once something has been done or said, it can't be taken back. The same is true of certain opportunities. This is why being intentional with your words and actions is so important.

Most often, it's words that are unleashed and then later regretted by the person who spoke them. While many things in life are outside of your control, the words you choose to speak isn't one of them. If you asked yourself before speaking, "How will this make them feel?" you will greatly reduce your chances of saying something you'll regret, and prevent the other person from feeling hurt. Sounds like a sure-fire way to test positive to me!

Do you regret anything you've said to another person? How can you make amends?

What are some ways you can prevent future regrets?

"It's not what we have in
our life, but who we have
in our life that counts."

- J.M. Laurence

Day 252

I f living through a global pandemic taught us anything, it's that the material things we have don't matter. It's the people in our lives that make us wealthy. I'm blessed beyond belief by the special people in my life, and I bet you are too.

The currencies we should pursue the most are love, relationships, and connection. A great way for you to test positive is expressing gratitude to those who encourage, love, and support you no matter what. Let them know how much you appreciate them!

In what way did living through a pandemic help you more deeply appreciate the special people in your life?

_____

_____

How many people can you say, "Thank you" to today?

_____

_____

"I love you.
You're probably thinking
'You don't even know me,'
but if people can hate for
no reason, I can love."

- Unknown

Day 253

Humans are great at many things, but I wish we weren't so good at judging others based only on what's visible on the surface. You can't really know someone just by hearing a few words, or observing a single reaction. People tend to be more complex than that.

If we're going to judge others, how about we judge them worthy of respect, love, and kindness? What if we give them the space to be imperfect and in need of encouragement? What a difference that would make in the world!

How does it make you feel when others judge you prematurely?

_____

_____

How can you support and encourage someone you don't know very well today?

_____

_____

"If standing up for yourself burns
a bridge, I have matches.
We ride at dawn."

- Unknown

Day 254

S tand up! It's uncomfortable and sometimes awkward, but you must define what you're willing to accept from others. Your life can be characterized by love and kindness, but the same can't be said of everyone. There are times when you have to stand by your boundaries and love others from a distance.

If you're being treated poorly at work, home, or anywhere else, it's time to make your stand. You might have to burn a bridge or two along the way, but if it means staying true to yourself, then do it. If you're putting out love and good vibes, you deserve the same!

In what way do you feel you are being treated poorly in your life?

_____

_____

How can you stand up for yourself today? New boundaries?

_____

_____

"People who wonder
whether the glass is half empty
or half full miss the point.
The glass is refillable.

- Simon Sinek

Day 255

E verything in life comes down to perspective. When things seem to be impossible, it's hard to maintain a sense of hope. It doesn't mean there's actually no hope, it's just how things look from a certain perspective.

It's okay to feel disappointment and fear. In fact, those are normal human emotions. If you allow them to rule your life and become a default viewpoint that'd be a problem, but if you see them as only temporary feelings that'll soon be replaced by possibility and joy, then your hold on hope remains strong!

How's your perspective today? Are you testing positive with hope and possibility?

_____

_____

What issues are you currently facing that could use a shift in perspective?

_____

_____

"When your intention
is clear, so is the way."

- Alan H. Cohen

Day 256

B
e intentional. I've said it several times in this book, and I'll keep saying it because it can't be overemphasized. Dreams and goals require focus and direction. Without them you'll get nowhere fast. So, what does it mean to be intentional? It means you make deliberate choices; your actions are done on purpose and not by chance. You know what you want and why you want it, and because of that you know what you must do.

You don't have to wake up and wonder what kind of day you're going to have. You're creating it! It's a great feeling, and when you feel great about yourself everything seems to work out better.

What's your intention for today?

_____

_____

How can you set yourself up for success every day? What routines can you put in place that'll help you create the life you desire?

_____

_____

How Safety Feels In The Body

- Relaxed nervous system.
- Deep belly breaths.
- Physical pains dissipate or ease.
- Thoughts feel clear and focused.
- Sleeping deeply.
- Feeling present, anchored, and steady.

Day 257

D o you feel safe in your life? The checklist on the left will help you do your own assessment and see if you're feeling emotionally and physically safe. When you do, everything in life just feels better—because it is better! If there's an area that's off, it's time to uncover the trigger that's making you feel uneasy.

Creating more peace in your life is possible, and removing certain triggers will go a long way in helping you do that. You may have to adjust your mindset, stop associating with certain individuals, or actively change your circumstances. Whatever must be done, you are capable of doing it. I believe in you!

How safe do you feel in your own life right now?

_____

_____

If you feel "off" in any way, what is triggering those feelings? What changes can you make?

_____

_____

Don't entertain negative energy.
Some situations will test your
patience and try to make you
overreact, overthink and respond
to things that don't deserve your
life force. Your attention is your
power. Don't feed what does not
add value to your life.
Conserve your energy."

- Unknown

Day 258

Protecting yourself from physical harm is almost automatic. Accidents, germs, injuries—avoiding these things doesn't require much thought. After all, physical protection is fairly obvious, but you know what isn't? Protecting your energy!

Your emotional health depends heavily on the kinds of energy you surround yourself with, as well as the energy you create. It's easy to get sucked into negative thoughts, conversations, and behaviors. Seldom do any of these things benefit you in any way. In fact, they do lots of harm to your physical and emotional health. When you encounter negativity, shift your focus onto that which is good. Give your attention only to those things that add value to your life and the lives of others!

Have you allowed negative energy to gain a foothold in your life? In what ways?

_____

_____

What steps can you take to protect your energy?

_____

_____

"If you hold your feelings back
and never give them legs to
run, then you will walk in circles
the rest of your life in regret."

- Alfa Holden

Day 259

I f I've said it once, I've said it a bazillion times: our issues live in our tissues! If you try to suppress negative or highly charged emotions like anger, guilt, regret, or fear, your body will pay a heavy price. What may begin as mild symptoms can progress to full on illness and even disease.

Release those feelings in healthy ways. Talk to a trusted friend, or seek help from a qualified professional. Do what it takes to process and experience your feelings, rather than merely suppressing them, and you'll significantly improve your relationships. Plus, you just might save your own life!

Are you suppressing any feelings and emotions?

_____

_____

What actions can you take to that will help you deal with, and release, your suppressed feelings?

_____

_____

"Sometimes we need a bridge and sometimes we are the bridge. No one I know has escaped troubled waters, rough seas and challenging, scary days. There are times in our lives when we could use a little help, and other times when we are given the chance to be that help for someone else."

- Paul Boynton

Day 260

No one is an island. Everyone goes through difficult times, and everyone faces scary situations. There are times when the person going through tough times is you, other times it's someone else, and we are either the bridge or in need of one.

One thing I find beautiful about having faced difficulties is that it equips you to help others when they're going through a hard time. We're walking in this life together, so let's be open to opportunities to offer a helping hand to someone in need, or gratefully accept a helping hand ourselves!

Can you remember a time when you needed a bridge? How about a time when you were the bridge for someone else?

_____

_____

Are you aware of someone who needs a little help right now? If it's you, who can you reach out to for some help?

_____

_____

"That's the problem with putting others first; you've taught them you come second."

- Anonymous

Day 261

A t first glance, today's quote may seem like it's implying that you're more important than other people. However, that's not what it's saying at all. What it's pointing out is that you're **just as important** as everyone else! We're often told that we should put other's needs before our own, and while that may be necessary on some occasions, doing it all of the time will deplete you and cause you to burn out.

Helping others is great, but you can't pour from an empty cup. You must make your needs a priority as well. Additionally, if you always put yourself last, you'll train others to treat you the same way. Take good care of yourself first, and then go help others!

Look closely. Are you putting yourself last in any of your relationships?

_____

_____

What are some ways you can put yourself in front of the line?

_____

_____

"You need to learn it, so
I took you through it."

- The Universe

Day 262

When you're going through a difficult time, it's freaking hard to imagine that any good could come from it. I've been there, and so have you, but here's the thing. If we take a good look at ourselves, we'll see strengths and abilities that we would've never developed had we not faced down challenges.

Personal growth and wisdom are the rewards for making it through the rough patches. Keep that in mind the next time a hard situation arises. You got this!

What strengths do you possess that came from making it through a tough time?

_____

_____

If you're in the middle of a rough patch right now, what lessons could you take away from it?

_____

_____

"Your life is a reflection of your thoughts. If you change your thinking, you change your life.

- Brian Tracy

Day 263

Your life is a mirror that's reflecting your inner world of thoughts. People and circumstances can definitely affect you, but they can't fully control your life. Only you have that power. The choices you make in life are directly influenced by how you think, and the way you think determines how you react to external influences.

Yes, it takes effort and time to change your thinking habits, but the good news is that it's possible! Take your power back by focusing on what you can control (your thoughts) and make intentional life choices. This is your life, create it!

What can you pinpoint in your life that's a direct result of your thoughts?

_____

_____

How can you begin training yourself to think differently?

_____

_____

"Look at your daily habits and ask yourself if they are causing you to evolve or revolve. Are you moving forward, or just moving in circles?"

- Unknown

Day 264

I t's easy to become complacent and accept the status quo. You got to a certain point by thinking and doing things in a certain way, but that'll only take you so far. As you grow and evolve, so must your thoughts and actions.

It's like going to the gym and doing the exact same exercises over and over. You'll achieve a certain level of fitness, but then you'll hit a plateau and your progress stalls. You could keep doing what you've always done, and go nowhere, or you could change your exercise habits and keep moving forward. Life works in the same way. If things have become stagnant, then it's time to make some changes!

What might keep you stuck on a plateau in any area of your life?

_____

_____

What changes can you make that will keep you moving forward?

_____

_____

"Food is not just calories, it is information. It talks to your DNA and tells it what to do. The most powerful tool to change your health, environment and entire world is your fork."

- Dr. Mark Hyman

Day 265

F ood may not be at the top of the list when you think of ways to transform your life, but it definitely should be! Today's quote says it perfectly. Food is much more than calories, it's literally affecting how you think, feel, and perform.

Just like your car requires a certain kind of fuel, your body needs to be supplied with proper nutrients if you want it to perform at optimum levels. To put it simply, what you eat matters!

How would you describe your health and physical performance?

_____

_____

What dietary changes can you make that will improve your health and well-being?

_____

_____

"You can't wait until life
isn't hard anymore before
you decide to be happy"

- Nightbirde

Day 266

Sometimes life is freaking hard! I'll be the first to tell you that testing positive is often easier said than done—but it can be done! The thing is, if you wait until everything is perfect in your life before being happy, then you're never going to be happy.

You don't have to lie to yourself and say all is well when it isn't, but keep things in perspective. Life can be hard at times, but it's still a beautiful experience. Look for the good, feel gratitude, and watch how quickly things turn around!

How's your outlook on life these days? Would you describe it as upbeat and positive?

_____

_____

What are three things you are most grateful for right this moment?

_____

_____

"Embrace and love
your body. It's the most
amazing thing you'll ever own."

- Unknown

Day 267

Many of us endeavor to not be judgmental toward others. I think that's a beautiful thing, but the way you think and behave toward yourself is just as important. While we're busy going easy on others, we judge our weight, wrinkles on our face, scars, or any number of other perceived imperfections. This has to stop.

I've worked very hard on this, especially since undergoing surgery for breast cancer. I make it a point to be grateful and appreciate my body. It has done so much for me, and continues to do so. Caring for it is a priority for me. After all, it's the least I could do. Make me a promise? Love and appreciate your body, and care for it to the best of your ability!

What is your attitude toward your body?

_____

_____

How can you express gratitude toward your body, and show it your appreciation?

_____

_____

"Destruction can feel like realignment if you shift your perspective and allow it to be."

- Unknown

Day 268

When something changes, especially if it's unexpected, it can jar you to the core. It could be a relationship, job, or even your health, but it can sometimes feel like your world is crumbling all around you. Surely there's nothing good that could come from it, right? Actually, yeah. It's possible!

What feels like destruction could also feel like transformation, you just have to shift your perspective. What happened could be a clue to something in your life that's doesn't align with your values, or is leading you further away from life goals. You don't have to ignore the fact that the situation hurts, but it could be a gift that happened to arrive wrapped in pain. This might be an opportunity to realign your life and your purpose!

What changes have you recently experienced that were painful?

_____

_____

Could the changes be clues or an opportunity? How so?

_____

_____

"Get into the habit
of asking yourself:

Does this support the
life I'm trying to create?"

- Unknown

Day 269

Autopilot works great for airplanes, but I've discovered it doesn't work very well as a lifestyle. Decisions made with little thought can often work against you, especially if you want to build your life in a certain way. Goals are reached one step at a time, and decisions are essential steps in the process.

Start by making intentional choices. Switch off autopilot and take hold of the controls. Before making a decision, ask yourself some key questions. "Why do I want to do this?" or "Will doing this take me closer to my goal, or further away?" Answering questions such as these will ensure you stay on track. It's your life, design it on purpose!

What are some decisions you've made on autopilot? Did they get you closer to your goals?

_____

_____

Are your upcoming decisions going to support the life you're trying to create? How?

_____

_____

"Hope can be a powerful force. Maybe there's no actual magic in it, but when you know what you hope for most and hold it like a light within you, you can make things happen, almost like magic."

- Laini Tavlor

Day 270

Hope is like a compass that leads you to the light, no matter the darkness that surrounds you. When it's lost, you'll lose more than your way—you'll lose the will to continue. As much as outward evidence may seem to indicate the contrary, hope will not abandon you!

When the dark times come and try to convince you all hope is lost, dig in your heels and hold fast. Remember why you started in the first place, and how far you've come. Break out your compass and run to the light!

What do you hope for, and what gets you through dark times?

_____

_____

In what ways have you experienced the power of hope?

_____

_____

"One thing I realized is that everything always ends up working out. Sometimes even better than you can imagine. Remember this when you feel like you're in a hard place or you feel like you're being challenged the most. Believe in where you're headed."

- Idil Ahmed

Day 271

When you're in the midst of difficulty, the hardest thing to remember is that it's temporary, and that you have what it takes to make it through. How do I know that? Because you've gotten through everything else! You're here to tell the tale, and share the wisdom you gained with others.

Good times may not last, but neither do bad times. Life is in a state of ebb and flow all the time, which is a good thing to keep in mind when things get tough. Believe in what you're doing, and believe in yourself!

Remember a time when things looked bleak, but turned out great? Write about your experience.

_____

_____

Are you experiencing a tough challenge right now? Do you believe in what you're doing? List all the reason why you're going to make it!

_____

_____

"I am blessed.
Today I will focus on all
that is right in my life."

- Unknown

Day 272

The world appears to have gone totally nuts, especially in the last few years. It seems there's bad news everywhere, and it starts to feel heavy after a while. How can you feel grateful and happy in the midst of it all? By realizing that everything is **not** bad, and that there's plenty of good still in the world! Understand that most media outlets thrive on negativity, which means you have to limit how much of that garbage you take in.

I'll never advise others to ignore what's going on in the world, but it's possible stay informed without bathing in negative information every day. Focusing on all that's wrong in the world won't change anything anyway, but do you know what does? Focusing on what's good in life! Feeling and expressing gratitude will literally change you, both mentally and physiologically. A positive change in you is contagious, and will spread to others. That's a great way to test positive right there!

How are you feeling? Mentally, spiritually, and physically? Has the negativity gotten to you?

_____

_____

Bring yourself back to gratitude. Name everything you can think of that makes you feel grateful. Focus on these things!

_____

_____

"Do more things that make
you forget your phone."

- Unknown

Day 273

How much screen time have you been clocking lately? You may have found yourself staring at your phone a lot more in the past couple of years, and so have millions of others. Of course, a pandemic and lockdowns made that all too easy to do. Now that things have begun to open up, can we let go of the habit? There's nothing wrong with checking your phone, but it's good to understand why it can be addictive. Studies have shown that phone activity causes your brain to release dopamine, making you feel good, which makes you want to do it even more. Then, a habit is born.

You know the best way to break a habit? Replace it with a healthy one! You can get the same benefits of dopamine in healthier ways, such as exercise, accomplishing a goal, listening to music, sleep, and meditation!

Are you spending a lot of time on your phone or watching TV? How has it impacted your sense of well-being?

_____

_____

What are some healthier habits you can implement in your life?

_____

_____

"Any relationship you have that could get ruined by having a conversation about your feelings, standards, and/or expectations wasn't really stable enough to begin with."

- Unknown

Day 274

Relationship stress can take years off of your life—literally. I'm not just talking about romantic relationships, but also friends, family, or coworkers. All stress is harmful, but the kind that comes from rocky relationships can be long-lasting and intense. Great care should be taken when choosing who you allow into your life, and just because you're related to someone doesn't mean you have to hang out with them.

Maybe it's time to stop settling and focus on relationships that are healthy, supportive, and allow you to be yourself. Genuine love is when you're loved for who you are—not who someone else thinks you should be!

Which of your relationships are creating stress in your life? Why?

_____

_____

What boundaries can you create, and with whom, that will decrease the amount of stress you're experiencing?

_____

_____

"It's not what you say to everyone else that determines your life it's what you whisper to yourself that has the greatest power."

- Robert T Kiyosaki

Day 275

Would you speak to others the way you speak to yourself? What if it were your best friend, child, or grandmother? Would you talk to them differently? I bet you'd choose your words carefully so they wouldn't be hurt, which is exactly the same care you should take when talking to yourself!

It's going to be tough to live a happy life if you're overcritical of yourself, or put yourself down on a regular basis. You love others only to the extent you love yourself, and others learn how to treat you based on how you treat yourself. Test positive today by having lots of positive self-talk!

How would you describe the way you talk to yourself?

_____

_____

Does your self-talk need a positive upgrade? What are some encouraging things you can say to yourself?

_____

_____

"Your boundaries matter even when people won't respect them. It's not your job to grow a thicker skin, or learn to put up with it, or make excuses for inappropriate behavior. It's your job to learn how to enforce your boundaries.

- Unknown

Day 276

D o you struggle with creating boundaries, setting limits, and speaking your truth? Being treated with respect, and being able to speak truthfully is not a privilege, or favor granted to you by someone else. IT IS YOUR RIGHT!

This applies to work, family, and romantic relationships. You teach people how you want to be treated by what you allow and accept, so be sure to teach them right!

What has stopped you from setting self-respecting boundaries with people in your family, workplace and friend group? Setting boundaries means saying no to disrespectful or unloving treatment.

_____

_____

What has held you back from setting boundaries in the past?

_____

_____

"The messenger can only deliver the message to those who are a vibrational match to the message. So don't stress yourself out saying things to people who can't hear you."

- Unknown

Day 277

I t's hard to test positive when people don't seem to "get" you, understand your feelings, point of view, or don't feel the same way about certain things. You might take it personally and it hurts sometimes.

But what if it's not personal, and they're simply not a vibrational match for **that particular message**? This gives you the space to let go of anger and resentment, and instead offer grace to the person who isn't "getting" it. You can only meet people where they are, not where you wish them to be. Understanding this puts you in such a different state!

If you were able to stop taking things personally from others, how would that affect your life?

_____

_____

Who are you harboring resentment toward because they didn't understand you or your viewpoint? Can you work on letting that go today?

_____

_____

"Pay attention to the things you are naturally drawn to. They are often connected to your path, passion, and purpose in life. Have the courage to follow them."

- Ruben Chavez

Day 278

We all have things that really light us up. I see this in my coaching clients and audiences all the time. As soon as I bring up certain topics, their faces light right up, their energy shifts, and even their body language changes. That's when I know we're onto something important!

Pay attention to that feeling, to the things that you're drawn to, and make you feel excited, happy, peaceful, and content. These are the things worthy of your time and attention. Pour your energy into them because they just might be tied to your purpose. Pursue them with boldness and courage! If you did that, how would your life transform in a week, month, or year?

What can you do today that lights you up, and fills you with excitement , joy, and peace?

_____

_____

What gets in the way of doing these things on a daily or weekly basis? How can you remove that barrier?

_____

_____

"Life is a matter of choices,
and every choice you
make makes you."

- John Maxwell

Day 279

Today is a great day to check in with yourself and see if your choices are leading you to become who you want to be, and taking you where you want to go. What's working for you, and what isn't? It can be easy to get into a rut and keep doing what you've always done, but it might be time for some new choices.

The ability to choose is a super power—YOUR super power! You can choose differently. The only question is, will you?

If you could change one thing in your life, what would you choose to be different?

_____

_____

What's holding you back from making different choices?

_____

_____

"When you judge another,
you do not define them,
you define yourself."

- Wayne Dyer

Day 280

It sure feels awful to be judged unfairly by someone doesn't it? I've experienced it before, and I bet you have too. The thing is, people often judge you without knowing anything about you or your situation. That's a truth worth remembering because it applies to us all.

It's easy to make snap judgements based only on what you see, but the chances of being wrong are high because you'll never know the full story. We get enough of that on social media, right? Besides, judging others says more about the one judging than anyone else. Spreading love is the only way in which you are guaranteed to be 100% right, 100% of the time!

Monitor how frequently you make judgements about others today, you might be shocked by how often this happens subconsciously. Make notes on how it goes!

_____

_____

Often, judging others is a reflection of the things we don't like in ourselves. What do you not like about yourself? Start working on being more loving and accepting of YOU and watch that spill over on to others.

_____

_____

"What mental health needs is more sunlight, more candor, and more unashamed conversation."

- Glenn Close

Day 281

Have you noticed how much easier it is to tell others about your physical aches and pains than it is to share with them how you feel emotionally? I am so blessed to have a tribe of people in my life who not only want to know, but are willing to listen.

Imagine if every workplace and family had people who genuinely wanted to know how others felt, made them feel safe to share, and were willing to listen. We're talking a global transformation! It may sound like a lofty goal, but it can start right now with you and me.

Take time today and ask someone how they're feeling emotionally, and listen with empathy and an open heart.

_____

_____

What stops you from being honest, with yourself and others, about how you're doing emotionally? Don't say you're fine when you're not.

_____

_____

"A healthy attitude is contagious but don't wait to catch it from others. Be a carrier."

- Tom Stoppard

Day 282

I am contagious. I'm a carrier too, but not always. I've said it before and I'll say it again before the end of this book—testing positive isn't about trying to be positive at all costs. You have to acknowledge and deal with the crap in life when it comes. You can be honest about how you're feeling, with yourself and those in your life whom you trust.

You have to work through low vibration emotions like anger, loss, grief, shame and doubt. By clearing those negative emotions, you make space for better things to move in. By practicing gratitude, you'll find your way back to the higher vibration emotions of love and joy. Then, you'll become a magnet for even more love and joy!

What negative emotions are you struggling to let go of, and what's holding you back from letting them go?

_____

_____

Gratitude is one way to find your way back to love and joy. What other strategies can you use?

_____

_____

"Every time you subtract negative from your life, you make room for more positive."

- Thurka

Day 283

We often hold on to people, things, or responsibilities that are no longer in our best interest. We hold on because it became our normal, and changing things can feel scary. If this sounds familiar, you're not alone. Deep down, you already know what's best for you.

You can't create a positive life when your life is full of things that feel negative! Please consider that it's only by letting go of that which does not serve you, that you can make room for that which does. I know it takes more courage to let go than it does to hold on, but you can do this!

Are there habits, people, or choices that are having a harmful effect on your life? How can you work on letting go?

_____

_____

When you have negative thoughts, try replacing them with positive ones. What are some negative thoughts you now hold? How can they be replaced with positive ones?

_____

_____

"One day you'll look back
and realize how hard it was,
and just how well you did."

- Charlie Mackesy

Day 284

Have you noticed how when you're in the middle of chaos, it starts to feel less chaotic after a while? It's not because the situation changed, but because you've changed. It may be that you've chosen to deal with things in healthier ways! What was once difficult becomes a little easier because you're wiser than you were at the beginning.

It's great day to look at look at yourself with a fresh perspective. Consider all that you've been through, acknowledge your strength, and celebrate all that you've become!

Look back over the past year, or even the last month. Can you see growth? In what ways have you changed or grown?

_____

_____

Looking ahead, what skills or strengths have you developed that'll help you through future challenges?

_____

_____

"When you ask someone how they are doing, do you really mean it? When you answer someone back how you are doing, are you really telling the truth?"

- Brady Quinn

Day 285

Testing positive is all about being intentional. So often, we automatically greet people by asking, "How are you?" Do we really want to know, or is it something said out of habit?

Being intentional in how you interact with others means you care. You ask how they're doing, because you really want to know. It's a conscious choice to put yourself in a position to help someone who may be hurting. It seems like it's simply a polite greeting, but it's a question that's powerful enough to change someone's life if asked with genuine empathy and compassion.

Practice being intentional, and interacting with others from a place of authenticity and intention. How can you show you really care?

_____

_____

Not only do we ask "How are you?" out of habit, we also tend to respond "Fine, thanks" in the same way. Why do you default to that? Practice telling people the truth—good or bad. Tell them how you really are, and why.

_____

_____

"Anger is a mask–it covers up your true feelings like fear, jealousy, frustration or powerlessness. It's a way of dealing with a situation when you haven't processed the real feelings behind it."

- Unknown

Day 286

I s it me, or have you noticed that tempers flare over the smallest things these days? Speaking out of anger is dangerous because you can't take back the words once you've let them go. It's so important to pause and try to understand where the anger is coming from before someone is hurt irreparably.

Your triggers are your teachers, so feelings of anger are a clue and an opportunity. What's really behind it? Anger is often a secondary emotion, so have the courage to find out what's driving it and talk about THAT. That way, you're much more likely to build a bridge to someone you feel angry with, instead of putting up a wall that may never come down.

Can you identify what emotion lies beneath your anger? Could it be fear or insecurity? Where's it coming from?

_____

_____

When you feel angry, can you pause and find out what the actual trigger is? Seldom is it the fact that no one emptied the dishwasher, or took your parking spot. It could be that you feel disrespected or unimportant for example.

_____

_____

"I believe the best way to activate genius within the immune system is by ingesting certain superherbs and superfoods, taking probiotics and cultured foods, minimizing toxic food exposure by eating pure organic raw-living foods, and making appropriate healthy lifestyle improvements."

- David Wolfe

Day 287

Did you know that your greatest defense against illness or disease is a robust immune system? There are many ways to keep build up your immune system. You probably know that it takes healthy food, exercise, and limited exposure to harmful chemicals, but you know what's just as important? Your thoughts!

Test positive by making some changes! Make the conscious choice to carefully consider what you put into your body, the amount of exercise you get, the people you spend time with, and the thoughts you focus your attention on every day. Ask yourself, "Does this enhance my immune system?" If you can't answer that question, THAT is you answer.

What can you do today to enhance your immune system?

_____

_____

What things do you need to **stop** doing that are clearly a threat to your immune system?

_____

_____

"Be the reason someone feels welcome, seen, heard, valued, loved, and supported."

- Unknown

Day 288

The ripple effect is real! When you intentionally choose how you're going to show up in the world, you're choosing what you want to experience. It's the law of attraction in action, and an energetic boomerang. What you send out comes back.

If you want to feel welcomed, loved, and understood, give those things to other people. That beautiful energy continues to expand and the ripple effect benefits everyone—including you!

How will you choose to show up in the world today? What would you like to experience?

_____

_____

Make a list of qualities you admire most in others. Start bringing those qualities into every situation and watch your life changes!

_____

_____

"If the words you spoke
appeared on your skin,
would you still be beautiful?"

- Auliq Ice

Day 289

We often censor the words we speak to others, and we do that because there are very real consequences to saying what we're thinking. But what about the words you say to yourself? Do you examine them as closely as the words you say to others? What if the words you spoke to yourself showed up on your skin? How do these words harm YOU? You were born with a perfect heart and soul. You didn't think of yourself as fat, stupid, messy, or not good enough. You learned those things from an outside source, and somehow "bought" the story.

Today, speak to the little girl or boy inside the way they deserve. Speak words of love, compassion, kindness, and confidence. We're all the same kind of amazing. Every. Single. One. Of. Us.

Write down some of the mean things you say about yourself and imagine saying those things to someone you love. Strike them out and speak truth about yourself. (eg. My eyes are beautiful, I'm strong, I'm smart).

_____

_____

What does it feel like to look into a mirror and practice saying something positive about yourself? It might feel weird at first, but it's so powerful!

_____

_____

"Surround yourself with the
people who love your crazy,
and a few that are even crazier."

- Unknown

Day 290

Who do you surround yourself with? Do they make you laugh? Do you love them, and do they love you back? Do they support you, or do they make you feel scared? Are you comfortable being yourself around them, or do you feel as though you're walking on eggshells?

Your external environment creates your internal environment, and vice versa. If you're surrounded by people who make you question your worth, that might be a reflection of how you're feeling about yourself. You teach people how to treat you by what you accept. Surround yourself with those who lift you up and treat you with love and respect. Those who laugh easily and make you laugh. You deserve that!

How do the people in your life make you feel?

_____

_____

Why do you allow others to treat you poorly? Is it fear of conflict, insecurity, or abandonment issues? Dig deep and challenge that irrational belief.

_____

_____

"You have not lived today
until you have done
something for someone
who can never repay you."

- John Bunyan

Day 291

oesn't it feel amazing to be THAT person for someone? If you ever need validation for your purpose on the planet, or your ability to make a difference in the lives of others, do something for someone with no expectation of a return. A small act of kindness can make a giant impact. It could be an encouraging word, a smile, compliment, or as simple as holding a door open for someone.

The energetic boomerang will bring back to you the same beautiful energy you give, and amplify it in ways you can't imagine. You're making a difference, and your value is infinite. Show others you feel the same is true about them.

What act of kindness can you do today for someone today?

_____

_____

Who made a huge difference in your life with an act of kindness?

_____

_____

"Men and women who
are doing inner healing
work is the new sexy."

- Unknown

Day 292

D o you find yourself in the same situation, living through the same drama with the same people, while experiencing disappointment, sorrow, and suffering? It kind of feels like you're in the movie *Groundhog Day* and living the same day over and over, doesn't it?

It's possible you're stuck in a particular way of living because of something inside of you that's attracting the same type of people or circumstances, which lead you to make similar choices. Over time, a pattern develops that keeps perpetuating itself. You can break the pattern by having the courage to do the necessary inner work. Find someone who can guide you through that process and bring healing to the areas of your life in which you've been wounded. The work you do on yourself is the most important work you'll do. It's not just the new sexy, it's the new strong!

What circumstances are you stuck in? Are there thought patterns contributing to your situation? This is crucial, so dig deep on this.

_____

_____

Can you recognize a pattern of settling in your life? What are you settling for that you should not accept?

_____

_____

"Ships don't sink because of the water around them. Ships sink because of the water that gets in them. Don't let what's happening around you get inside you and weigh you down."

- Unknown

Day 293

You can't always change circumstances, but you always get to decide how you respond to them. It requires some self-discipline, but often the only thing you can change is you!

When your vibrational frequency is lowered because you're angry, frustrated, or filled with regret, you'll attract more of the same. Do whatever it takes to keep the garbage surrounding you "out there" so it doesn't sink you. Instead, shift your focus to things that raise your frequency, like love, gratitude, and joy!

How can you shift your thinking so you feel more gratitude, joy, and love?

_____

_____

What keeps you stuck in those low frequency, negative emotions?

_____

_____

"Work hard.
Drink coffee.
Stay sweet.
Enjoy life."

- Unknown

Day 294

Don't allow what's going on in the world around you to take away your sweetness, kindness, and empathy. Your joy and sweetness will wane if you get caught up in the negativity. You don't have to pretend it doesn't exist, just don't feed it all of your attention. There's still a lot of good and positive things in the world, so focus on those things!

Find your joy. Create it for yourself and others. Like the old adage says, "Joy shared is joy doubled." That still rings true!

What can you do today that brings you joy?

_____

_____

What can you plan this week that creates joy for your friends, family, or co-workers. It doesn't have to be extravagant, just something meaningful. Take the family on a hike, organize a lunch with some friends at work, or send flowers to a close friend! What are some more ideas?

_____

_____

"Last week, I found
myself saying I was 'stressed.'
This week, I said I am 'under
divine pressure because I'm
birthing something great.'
Narrative shift."

- Unknown

Day 295

Testing positive is about your perspective, and perspective is everything, isn't it? The way you look at things determines the kind of energy you allow those things to create. People, circumstances, it doesn't matter. The energy you create determines your life experience.

Controlling your perspective controls the energy. Do you see the power of a mind shift? You can directly influence what you attract into your life. When you shift things and step into your power, you can create the life you want!

What needs shifting in your perspective today?

_____

_____

How can you help those around you shift their perspective? Be careful not to invalidate a negative perspective, simply invite people to see the possible in the impossible.

_____

_____

"Perfectionism is self-abuse
of the highest order."

- Anne Wilson Schaef

Day 296

Do you have impossibly high standards? Are you hesitant to take action because everything isn't perfect? If this sounds familiar, you might be a perfectionist. Are you ready to let that go? Let's stop the abuse and find a little grace and self-love!

Working toward excellence is great, but feeling like you have to be perfect (whatever that is) will make you miserable and prevent you from creating great work. You don't have to achieve something, or BE anything in order to be worthy of respect, kindness, love, and compassion. You're more than enough already!

Let's remember this is also true for the people around you.

Are you holding yourself to impossibly high standards? In what areas of your life?

_____

_____

Are you holding others to an impossibly high standard? Why?

_____

_____

«When a flower doesn't bloom, you fix the environment in which it grows, not the flower.»

- Alexander Den Heijer

Day 297

Are you happy? If you can't immediately answer yes, what needs to change? Paradoxically, we look outside ourselves in an attempt to find happiness, but the answer doesn't lie in our external environment, but within our internal environment.

Your self-talk, thoughts, and even your health, all come together to create an environment through which you experience life. It's your heart and soul that's the flower living inside of that environment. If you poison it with negativity and poor health habits, you won't be able to bloom.

Time for a little environmental therapy!

In what ways are you seeking happiness outside of yourself? Is it working?

_____

_____

Make a list of all of the things you love about yourself, or that others love about you. Focus more on expanding those things!

_____

_____

"All emotion are acceptable.
All behavior is not."

- Dr Lauren Fogel Mersy

Day 298

T oday's a great day to test positive by paying extra attention to how you're showing up in the world. There's no question that life can be stressful at times, but how does it manifest in your life? It's okay to feel the emotions, but it's not okay to lash out on the people around you! Being stressed doesn't mean you get a free pass to treat others poorly, and you don't have to give a free pass to others for treating you that way. We all must work through our own s**t without leaving casualties in our wake.

While it's okay to not be okay sometimes, do your best to avoid making others feel that way too.

What can you do to ensure the stress you're experiencing doesn't affect the people around you?

_____

_____

How can you create healthy boundaries with the people in your life to prevent them from taking their stress out on you? How can you support them without taking on their problems?

_____

_____

"If we allow our thoughts to
arise and dissolve by
themselves, they will pass
through our mind as a bird
flies through the sky,
without leaving a trace."

- Dilgo Khyentse Rinpoche

Day 299

Thoughts are difficult to control sometimes. Think about that for a moment. If you think of telling someone off, it's pretty easy to not act on it because there would be consequences. However, the real challenge lies with preventing the thought from showing up in the first place.

The truth is that everyone has intrusive thoughts. What you do with them is what's important. A thought can only survive if you feed it the energy of your attention. If you starve it, it passes through your mind and dissolves. Negative thoughts that receive your attention will grow in power, potentially causing physiological, biochemical, and energetic changes in your body!

Remember, you attract what you think about the most!

Write down any persistent negative thoughts, and then write down a positive alternative thought. For example: "I hate when it rains." Replace with: "The trees are loving all this rain!"

_____

_____

How many negative thoughts do you have in a day. Are you surprised by the number?

_____

_____

"Sometimes healing has nothing to do with the people who've hurt you. Sometimes healing is apologizing to yourself for all the bullshit you made yourself believe."

- r.m. drake

Day 300

E veryone carries with them a story from childhood that gets reinforced as you search for things to fit the narrative. Your story might be a fear of abandonment, and now all of your relationships are superficial and shallow. Or you might have, as I did, a story of disempowerment which attracts bullies disguised as friends, partners, or coworkers.

Those stories are NOT your reality! They are not YOU! Let go of those old stories and accept this one: You are human and worthy of every good thing possible, just as every other human!

What story from childhood is affecting you now as an adult?

_____

_____

Find some evidence that contradicts your old story. For example: If your story is that you're stupid, can you think back to experiences where you were clearly wise? I know you can! Write about it below.

_____

_____

"In the end, people will judge you anyway. So don't live your life impressing others. Live your life impressing yourself."

- Eunice Camacho Infante

Day 301

Quit playing small for fear of what others will think or do! Worrying about what everyone else thinks is like being in handcuffs—literally bound, and in many ways, powerless. You're not required to seek the approval of others for how you live your life. Go ahead and give yourself permission to stop.

Be unapologetically you!

Do you feel the need to seek approval from anyone in your life? Why?

_____

_____

Can you think of a time when you deliberately did the opposite of what people were expecting? What were the results of doing things your way and not for the approval of others?

_____

_____

"Everybody comes from the same source. If you hate another human being, you're hating part of yourself."

-Elvis Presley

Day 302

I don't know about you, but I like to making deposits into my good karma bank as often as possible, so if I need to make a withdrawal I've got equity! Being a good human, putting love and kindness vibes into the world, does a lot more than invite good karma, it actually changes you physiologically!

Acts of kindness create a surge of serotonin, and who doesn't need more good mood fluid? Then comes the bonus, a beautiful ripple effect in everyone who witnesses the act of kindness!

What can you do today to create some good karma for yourself?

_____

_____

How can you release past hurts and thoughts of payback? Wishing bad karma for others only attracts it for yourself anyway. Silently thank those people for the lessons you learned and move on with love.

_____

_____

"Surround yourself with
beautiful and positive
people, who love you and
believe in you."

- Bryant McGill

Day 303

Today's a great day to focus on those that inspire, encourage, love, and support you. Make an effort to connect with those people who raise your vibrational frequency. You'll attract even more people who will support and inspire you, as you do the same for them!

For this to be even more effective, consider limiting or eliminating relationships that aren't contributing to your highest good. It's your life, and you decide who to associate with!

Think about some any relationships in your life that might be toxic, or unhealthy. What's holding you back from letting go?

_____

_____

Who can you connect with that'll raise your vibrational frequency? Reach out to them today!

_____

_____

"Repeat after me:
It's not my responsibility to
heal, save, punish or
control other people."

- Unknown

Day 304

Anyone who has ever attended one of my presentations on stress has heard me say this; "We create most of our own stress." That's right, as much as we'd like to blame others, we decide how much stress we're going to live with. If that stings a little, pause and consider the power in that statement. If you're the one who creates the stress, then YOU can stop it!

Today's a great day to drop expectations for healing, punishing, or saving others. You can only do those things for yourself, and when you do, you can then guide others in the process!

In what way do you create your own stress? Why?

_____

_____

How can you deal with the chronic stress in your life?

_____

_____

„When someone helps you and they are struggling too, that's not help, that's love."

- Unknown

Day 305

When you're going through a difficult time, it's natural to become a bit self-centered. Sometimes, you might turn inward in order to find the strength to push through, but you may still need help from someone else. Do you have a friend who helped you through a rough patch, even while they were going through one themselves?

Test positive today by acknowledging someone who has been there for you, even though they had their own struggle. Any person who can give compassion, support, and empathy while in the midst of their own difficulties is a true gift in your life!

Who do you need to acknowledge today for always being there for you? Can you make some time to do that, preferably in person?

_____

_____

Who can you be there for today? Can you offer support and help?

_____

_____

"We don't stop playing because we grow old; we grow old because we stop playing."

- George Bernard Shaw

Day 306

Today's a great day to focus on adding some fun to your life. If you take the time to rest, relax, and recharge, you can directly impact your health! When you shut off your stress response and activate your parasympathetic nervous system, it allows you to create better health instead of symptoms and disease.

Do something fun today!

How can you add some fun, relaxation or recharging to your day?

_____

_____

Can you make fun and relaxation a daily priority? How will you do it, what time of day, and where? If you can answer those questions it may help you deal with any barriers that might come up.

_____

_____

"The only difference between a good day and a bad day is your attitude."

- Dennis Brown

Day 307

You may not always be in control of circumstances in life, but you're always in control of your attitude and response. Don't give anyone else the power to dictate your reactions or your attitude. Choose to focus on the good, and enhance your biology, which specifically supports a healthy immune system— your greatest defense against illness!

Remember, I'm not saying that you ignore or suppress negativity. I'm saying it's best to learn how to deal with it. Otherwise your issues will live in your tissues!

What do you focus on the most: Everything that's going wrong, or everything that's going right? How can you make a mental shift?

_____

_____

What's the most effective way you've found to deal with negative emotions?

_____

_____

"Great things never come
from comfort zones."

- Unknown

Day 308

Choosing growth is a great way to test positive! Growth does not come from trying to maintain the status quo—that can actually be incredibly unhealthy. It's all too easy to become used to something that isn't good for you at all!

Today, do something different. Something that inspires you, makes you happy, and maybe even scares you a little. It doesn't have to be extravagant. Choose something different for dinner, take your team meeting outside, or join an exercise class. Be brave and see what's on the other side of your comfort zone!

What will you do to change things up today?

_____

_____

Are there areas in your life where you've attempted to maintain the status quo? Why? Are you ready to shake things up?

_____

_____

"Staying quiet to avoid external conflict simply transmutes the conflict inward. For the sake of 'keeping the peace' we create a battle inside."

- Unknown

Day 309

D ig deep, be bold, and work to address conflicts in the most respectful way you can. Swallowing anger, resentment and fear will make you sick. As I often say, your issues live in your tissues, and the more you suppress what should be addressed and expressed, the more dangerous it becomes physiologically.

What conflict do you need to find the courage to address and with whom?

_____

_____

What can you do to avoid conflict in your relationships? You may find, in some relationships, it's impossible to prevent. Some people become addicted to the drama of a fight. These relationships might be ones to let go of, or set boundaries with.

_____

_____

"Instead of judging a star
for falling, we make a wish.
Let's do that for humans too."

- Unknown

Day 310

Judgment can be insidious and we often don't realize we're doing it. It comes in many forms, and I've certainly been the victim of it several times. Maybe you have too.

Here's the thing, no one likes to be wrong. Yet, when we resort to judgment the probability of being wrong is very high. You seldom know the whole story, so making accurate assumptions is unlikely at best. It's a sure way to bring distress into a family or workplace. When everyone is treated with empathy and respect, we create an environment of harmony and peace—which means less stress for everybody! Instead of gossiping about the difficulties someone is experiencing, send them love and good wishes. After all, at some point you could be the one in need.

Who in your life are you judgmental about? Look for common ground and ways to help.

_____

_____

How will you respond if someone comes to you with gossip about another person? Can you see that by allowing it, you are condoning it?

_____

_____

"Stop the dreaming, hoping, wishing, wanting, waiting, and just make the leap."

- Unknown

Day 311

Do you have a bucket list, things you wish for, or hope to accomplish in your lifetime? I did—until I was diagnosed with cancer. Being diagnosed with cancer made me realize that I was so done with my bucket list. I was done with waiting and wishing. It was time to start DOING!

Tomorrow is never promised, so I encourage you to live today as if it were your last. Time is your most precious asset. Dream your big dreams, but don't stop there. Take the leap!

What's on your bucket list that you'd like to put on your "Let's do it now" list?

_____

_____

How can you keep the momentum going once you have completed the first thing?

_____

_____

"Funny how your quality of life improves dramatically when you surround yourself with good, intelligent, kind-hearted, and positive loving people."

- Unknown

Day 312

Y ou become your environment. That includes your friends, family, colleagues, and coworkers. If negativity dominates your environment, you'll absorb that energy and begin to take on the same characteristics. It takes time, but it'll happen.

Beyond the obvious problem of developing a negative attitude, is the impact on your health that comes with a negative mindset. You can't just "green smoothie" your way out of a toxic environment. Surround yourself with people who enhance or maintain your well-being and health.

Can you identify sources of negative energy in your environment? Think about people, physical surroundings, and your mindset.

_____

_____

How can you set healthy boundaries, with yourself and others, in order to protect your energy and maintain a positive environment?

_____

_____

"Never own a disease. Reduce the amount of time that you talk about being ill. Refuse to allow illness a place in your consciousness."

- Unknown

Day 313

Thoughts become things! You've read that a few times in this book and you've probably said it yourself. Do you know it applies to everything? When I was diagnosed with cancer in 2020, I refused to utter the words, "I have cancer."

Now, saying those words didn't make the cancer disappear, but it did help me to not adopt it as my identity. I wholeheartedly refused to BECOME the disease. That mindset also applies to labels like "I'm stupid, unlovable, incapable, languishing, broke" and so on. The life you want to create for yourself begins with choosing your own thoughts!

Do you have negative thoughts on repeat? What are they?

_____

_____

If you're ready to challenge those negative thoughts and trade them for something more positive, write it down. Examples: Instead of saying "I'm broke," say "I have enough money for what I need." Remember, thoughts become things!

_____

_____

"Believe.
There are angels among us."

- Unknown

Day 314

Has it ever occurred to you that you could be the "someone" another person has been praying for? A few years ago, I reconnected with an old high school friend who told me I was the reason he was still alive. I had no idea! He was my friend and I loved him, and that's all it took to make the difference.

The reason I share that is to demonstrate that your act of kindness, compassion, or willingness to listen, might be an answered prayer for someone who really needs it. YOU could be their angel. Dig into your divinity today.

Watch for opportunities to be someone's angel today. Who can you offer a smile, helping hand, or a genuine "How are you?"

_____

_____

If someone has been THAT person for you, how can you let them know today? Let them know how grateful you are!

_____

_____

"The best kind of people are the ones that come into your life and make you see sun where you once saw clouds. The people that believe in you so much, you start to believe in you too. The people that love you simply for being you. The once in a lifetime kind of people."

- Unknown

Day 315

I t's important to have relationships that bring joy, safety, peace, and love. This is such a beautiful way to test positive! When you surround yourself with people who radiate love and light, it amplifies the love and light inside you. Vibrating at that higher frequency becomes contagious, and it attracts more experiences to keep that vibrational energy high.

Now, if you don't want that in your life—carry on looking for the clouds while the rest of us bask in the sun!

Who are the people in your life who radiate love and light? Spend time with them today, even if it's just a few messages back-and-forth. The whole day will feel different!

_____

_____

If you're having a rough day, or going through a tough time in your life, who is your one "go to" person and why?

_____

_____

"Choose peace
over drama.
Distance over
disrespect."

- Unknown

Day 316

W ho loves a good drama? Me too! However, I only enjoy it when it's on Netflix or live theater, not in my day-to-day life, thank you very much! Another word for drama is stress. Today's a great day to test positive by doing everything you can to create a stress-free, drama-free, peaceful day.

You may have to walk away from someone, or something, in order to keep your peace intact, but be intentional about the kind of day you want to have and go create it!

What do you need to do in order to minimize drama and stress in your life today?

_____

_____

If there's long-term or chronic stress in your life, what's holding you back from tackling this?

_____

_____

"Appreciate the people who touch your life with kindness and make it better."

- Unknown

Day 317

Gratitude, love, appreciation—these are all high frequency emotions. Everything about your life improves when you have more of these. There's a universal law that'll ensure success: **The more appreciation, gratitude, and love you put out into the world, the more you get back in return!**

It's a simple concept, but challenging for us at times, especially if things are tough. Here's how you can test positive today. There are people in your life who touch your life with kindness, so let them know how much you appreciate them and why. Then, sit back and watch the magic begin!

List five people you're grateful for, and why. Send them each a text or give them a call to let them know how you feel.

_____

_____

Make a list of things you love and appreciate about yourself. Read that list to yourself every morning for the next week and observe how it shifts your mood.

_____

_____

"Stress, anxiety and depression are caused when we are living to please others."

- Paulo Coelho

Day 318

Please don't misunderstand the message in the quote. I'm not referring to clinical anxiety or depression. I'm referring to the fact that you can never be happy or free of the power of these negative states of being, if you live for the approval of others.

The most important love you'll ever find is the love you have for yourself. You teach others how you want to be loved, so when you love yourself, the people you attract into your life will love you the same way. Choose you!

Whose approval are seeking with your behavior? Can you let this go?

_____

_____

What have you taught others about how you want to be loved? If you allow people to treat you disrespectfully remember this: what you permit, you promote.

_____

_____

"In order to save myself,
I must destroy first the
me I was told to be."

- Unknown

Day 319

How do you talk to yourself about yourself? What labels have you given yourself, or accepted from others? Don't limit yourself, or accept what others have told you—that's how you can test positive today.

YOU ARE NOT A LABEL!

You're magical and you have unlimited potential. You just simply need to understand that no one can grow or thrive within a negative environment. Speak with love and self-compassion **TO** yourself and **ABOUT** yourself, and watch yourself grow!

What labels do you use to refer to yourself? Which of these labels have come from others, which have come from you? Are they true?

_____

_____

Let go of labels! Instead, make a list of ten positive qualities you possess. Try to bring these qualities into your day.

_____

_____

"We want instant lunch, instant cure, instant miracles, instant salary, instant success–instant everything. This instant civilization, we have obsessed with, has made us grow a tad too impatient in virtually everything about life. And, of course, that doesn't serve us so well."

- Boniface Sagini

Day 320

We live in a world obsessed with instant gratification. We can get food, information, and just about anything else, with the push of a button or a voice command. We get used to it and expect everything to work that way. But, it doesn't.

It doesn't work like that in relationships, workplace culture, or in the pursuit of goals. It's a slippery slope when we apply that kind logic to such things. Things that matter always take time, patience, intention, and sustainable effort every day. Things worth having are worth the effort and the wait.

What changes would you like to make in your life? Are you willing to put in the time, patience, intention and daily, sustainable effort?

_____

_____

Over the next week, rather than waking up and wondering how the day will go, try this; "Today is going to be a _____ day" and be INTENTIONAL about creating the day you WANT! How will you fill in the blank?

_____

_____

"When you replace
'Why is this happening to me?' with
'What is this trying to teach me?'
everything shifts."

- Unknown

Day 321

S**t happens. And sometimes it's some bad, unthinkable stuff. But being feeling like a victim is disempowering. You may not be able to control the circumstances, but you can control your reactions and thereby your physiology. How you react creates opportunity or hopelessness.

As a health coach, I spend a lot of time coaching people through the process of finding hope when things seem hopeless. Hope is a currency, and freedom comes with understanding the lessons that lie beneath experiences. Absolutely everything in my life improved when I finally learned and understood the lesson that came with a diagnosis of cancer in 2020.

What are you learning?

What lessons have hard and difficult times taught you, and were so valuable that you carry them with you still?

_____   _____

_____

A great way to create hope is to change your words. The next time you find yourself saying, "I can't," try asking yourself, "How can I?" How will that change your perspective?

_____

_____

"Do not speak badly of yourself, for the warrior that is inside you hears your words and is lessened by them. You are strong and you are brave. There is a nobility of spirit within you."

- David Gemmell

Day 322

Isn't it time to let go of self-criticism? Celebrate all that you are instead of focusing on what you are not. You teach others how to love you. If you're horrible to yourself, others may do the same.

I often ask my coaching clients, " Would you say to others all the things you say to yourself? If not, why not? Is it because those things would be hurtful?" Change what's going on **inside** of you so that what's happening **outside** of you can also change!

Every time you have a self-critical thought today, stop yourself and exchange it for a genuine self-loving thought. How you do that?

_____

_____

It's time to stop the self-abuse and self-criticism, from yourself and from others. Who in your life do you need to call out for the things they say to you? Find the courage to do that.

_____

_____

"When you're not used to being confident, confidence feels like arrogance. When you're used to being passive, assertiveness feels like aggression. When you're not used to getting your needs met, prioritizing yourself feels selfish. Your comfort zone is not a good benchmark."

- Dr. Vassilia

Day 323

Your "comfort zone" isn't where the magic happens. Ever! It's a place to rest, but it's not really a place for thriving. It's a place where most everything is familiar to you, and when you begin moving out of it everything feels weird, different, and **uncomfortable**.

But growth is like that. Embrace it. Step out. The life you dream of is waiting!

In what areas of your life are you stuck in a comfort zone?

_____

_____

Fear of _____ is keeping you stuck in your comfort zone. What goes in the blank?

_____

_____

"You let your bad days affect you too much. You don't let your good days affect you enough. Fix that."

- Unknown

Day 324

It's too easy to get stuck on the negative! Why does the human brain work that way? Your brain is designed to keep you alive, and it does that by continuously scanning your environment for threats. In some ways you could say that it's hard-wired to look for the negative. That means you need to be much more diligent about looking for the good things.

This kind of perspective shift, the desire to test positive, requires energy, attention, and intention, and it's so worth it!

When you notice yourself getting stuck on the negative, make the shift to something more positive. Example: Instead of saying, "It's raining today, and my car is going to get filthy!" Say something like this: "It's raining today, and my lawn is loving it!" How else can you make the shift?

_____

_____

Do you have a negative Nelly or Ned in your life? If so, how can you limit your exposure to them. Negativity is contagious!

_____

_____

"If you don't have time for things that matter, stop doing things that don't."

- Courtney Carver

Day 325

As an international speaker, I have the opportunity to speak with people from all around the world, and I've noticed a common thread woven through our conversations. It goes something like, "I want to be healthier and happier, but I just don't have time."

Really?!?

If you don't take time for your wellness, you'll be forced to take time for your illness. What matters more to you? I take this same message into businesses, and it can have a dramatic effect on the bottom line. When people are well, they come to work! Not only that, they also work safer and are more productive.

Every aspect of your life improves if you make the time to be well.

How can you invest in your health and happiness today?

_____

_____

How can you remove the "I don't have time" barrier?

_____

_____

"You find a way. You do whatever it takes…..if change is what you truly want, then you find a way. You do whatever it takes. No point in complaining if you aren't willing to take the steps needed to be taken that lead down the path of growth and towards a place of new beginnings."

- Madame K Poetess

Day 326

Test positive by declaring a "no complaints day!" Have you noticed that complaining about something never changes it? It does however change YOU, and not for the better.

Physiologically, the negative energy that comes from complaining, causes a biochemical cascade of harmful substances to flood your body. This increases inflammation, and it's harmful to your overall well-being. Plus, energy acts like a magnet. What you regularly feel or experience, you will attract. Focus on what's right in your life, and if something isn't right, fix it! Everything else changes when YOU do.

Take a moment and consider how often you complain during an average day. Are you surprised?

_____

_____

For fun, put a dollar in a jar for every complaint you utter for the next week. At the end of the week, donate the jar of money to a charity of your choice. While your complaints may not have done you any good, you can take the lesson learned and turn it into something good for a charity dear to your heart. How much money do you think you'll collect?

_____

_____

"Self-care is how you
take your power back."

- Lalah Delia

Day 327

Do you remember thinking of self-care as taking time for a bath, eating a healthy meal, or going for a walk? I used to believe that was self-care, and it was—before 2020. Self-care means so much more to me now!

You cannot green smoothie your way out of a toxic state of chronic stress! Self-care is much more. It means working through trauma responses, setting boundaries (and sticking to them), discovering your triggers, asking for help, moving out of your comfort zone, and more. It's about making YOU a priority for a change.

Are you ready to take your power back?

What acts of self-care, that'll truly settle your nervous system, can you dive into today?

_____

_____

Can you also focus on tackling the source of the chronic stress in your life? What would that look like?

_____

_____

"Learn to forgive people
and release them. Life
feeds back truth to people
in its own way and time."

- Unknown

Day 328

I t's hard to forgive! I'm not suggesting giving people a pass for cruelty, meanness or abuse. Choosing to forgive is not saying it's okay, it's about releasing the death grip negative emotions have on you.

What helps me is finding an explanation for their behavior, not an excuse. It helps create a bit of empathy which makes forgiveness much easier. Forgiveness is not just something you do for others, it's for your own well-being too. It frees you from being a hostage to the past. Oh, while you're working on forgiving others, forgive yourself too!

Who do you need to forgive? Make a list of people, and imagine yourself talking to each of them and finding a way to forgive them. If appropriate, speak to some directly, but even simply visualizing this will change your physiology.

_____

_____

Do you need to forgive yourself? For what? Focus on this until you feel free from unforgiveness.

_____

_____

"I am blessed.
Today I will focus on all
that is right in my life."

- Unknown

Day 329

Testing positive is about focusing your attention on what you have, not on what you don't have. When you focus on all that's good and positive in life, it helps create the beautiful energy to attract more things to feel grateful and positive about.

Thoughts become things, and changing your thoughts will change your reality!

How does spending time with someone who's gift is looking on the bright side and finding the lesson in adversity, affect you? What can you learn from their approach to life?

_____

_____

What are you proud of yourself for doing and feeling during difficult times? Make a list! For example, I used to feel like a victim during dark times in my life, but I'm proud to say that I no longer feel that way!

_____

_____

"You are not a machine.
Your **BEST** will look
different each day, and
that's totally okay!"

- Unknown

Day 330

W e expect ourselves to be the same every day. Why? And why do we expect the same from others? We won't be the same every single day, and neither will anyone else. To expect otherwise is a set up for disaster!

Your "best" is influenced by so many things, and some of them are outside of your control. However, the way you respond is always within your control. Cut yourself and others some slack and watch your stress diminish and your peace increase!

Keep your expectations realistic. Example: if you didn't sleep well, don't expect yourself to perform the same at the gym. Name a few ways you can do this today.

_____

_____

Give others the same grace you give yourself. You never know for sure what's going on in their lives. Who can you cut some slack for today?

_____

_____

"When you ask the universe to go to the next level, don't be surprised when every person preventing progress is removed from your life."

- Unknown

Day 331

Sometimes, bad things happen. Lovers go their separate ways, friends leave, or working relationships come to an end. You wonder why, but there's no obvious answer. Stand fast, my friend, because sometime in the future you just might see how your personal growth skyrocketed afterwards!

One of those relationships could've been an anchor that held you down and prevented your growth. Fear not, because progress can be painful at times, but it's worth it!

Can you think of a relationship that limited your personal growth How did things change after the relationship ended?

_____

_____

Are you allowing a current relationship to be an excuse to not change and grow? If so, why?

_____

_____

"Unexpressed emotions will never die. They are buried alive and will come forth later in an uglier ways."

- Sigmund Freud

Day 332

Our issues live in our tissues! To test positive, you'll have to find the courage to face the rage, fear, disappointment and loss you've experienced. Everything changes when you do that, but everything also changes if you don't.

I once had a client who felt they had failed at everything they tried to achieve in life. We were able to trace that emotion back to their relationship with their mother who always said, "You will never succeeded at anything." She was right, because my client believed her and swallowed the rage. I asked my client if they had elevated liver enzymes, and they did, but their doctor could not figure out why. I knew that anger stays in the liver and makes people sick.

It's time to unload suppressed emotions. You can talk about them with a trusted friend, or qualified professional, but you deserve to be out from under their power and experience freedom and peace.

What physical symptoms could be tied to specific emotions?

_____

_____

What will you do to resolve some of these issues that are living in your tissues? How can you move the energy out?

_____

_____

"We have no control over who people think we are. So don't worry. If they want to hate a fictional version of you that lives in their mind, let them. Don't drain yourself trying to be understood by people who insist on not understanding you. Keep your cup full. Go to the kindness."

- Matt Haig

Day 333

I t's time to stop letting people get under your skin. It doesn't hurt them, but it sure harms you physiologically by putting you into the stress response.

Some people will never get you, a few don't want to get you, and others have their own agenda. However, they decide to think of you isn't your problem anyway. Send them some love and let it go!

Today, make it a point to keep away from people who know how to push your buttons, and are happy to do so. Give yourself a reprieve and enjoy feeling great! How can you make this a habit?

_____

_____

How can you tackle this issue long-term? You may need to set some respectful and loving boundaries with anyone who likes to push your buttons.

_____

_____

"The more you praise and celebrate your life, the more there is in life to celebrate."

- Oprah Winfrey

Day 334

Test positive today with some self-celebration! You deserve it! It's easy to forget how much s**t you've actually been through and survived! Heck, sometimes you even thrived as a result of awful experiences. You are so strong!

When hard times come, and they will, you can either get bitter or better. Celebrate everything you've weathered, and look back on your personal growth and smile. Find some gratitude for all the lessons learned and wisdom earned!

List all the things you not only survived, but found a way to thrive through it. Celebrate the victories and the lessons!

_____

_____

When feeling depleted or overwhelmed, remind yourself of how many times you've succeeded in overcoming tough times. Can you think of a few personal examples?

_____

_____

"You can't always have a good day, but you can always face a bad day with a good attitude."

- Unknown

Day 335

Testing positive doesn't mean putting on rose-colored glasses and ignoring reality. What it means is redirecting your focus to the good things in your life. This brings forth feelings of gratitude, which helps create good health, instead of symptoms and disease. Plus, gratitude is the key to attracting more good things!

Tough times create opportunities for growth, and you have a 100% success rate for getting through tough times!

Can you think of a recent situation when you wondered if you'd make it through? What helped you get through?

_____

_____

If you're going through a hard time right now, try imagining what you might say about the experience three months from now. What growth might you experience?

_____

_____

"A positive attitude causes a chain reaction of positive thoughts, events and outcomes. It is a catalyst and it sparks extraordinary results."

- Wade Boggs

Day 336

Who doesn't love to be around people with an upbeat and positive attitude? Their energy just feels good and it's magnetic. Emotions like love, joy, and gratitude have a high frequency that attract and amplify those feelings.

Of course, the opposite is also true. The lower frequency emotions, like anger, doubt, and fear will attract like-frequency feelings and experiences. If you want your life to change for the better, it begins with changing your internal emotional state. It's an inside job!

Have you had a recent experience with emotional chain reactions? What were they and how would you deal with them differently?

_____

_____

How could you make your internal emotional state positive today?

_____

_____

"When writing the story of your life, don t let anyone else hold the pen."

- Unknown

Day 337

W hy do you do the things you do? That's a great question to ask yourself periodically. Are you doing what YOU want to do, or what you think OTHERS want or expect you to do? Trying to live up to someone else's expectations is a recipe for disaster. Not only do you dismiss your own needs, you seldom succeed at pleasing others anyway.

Be unapologetically you! As my soul sister, Michelle Mras, always says, "It's your life, live it your way!"

Are you living life to please others, or meet their expectations? What's driving you to do that?

_____

_____

What's something you'd really like to do or experience, but you think wouldn't be supported by the people you care about most? How will you deal with that in order to accomplish what you really want to do?

_____

_____

"When you can't control
what's happening, challenge
yourself to control how you
respond to what's happening.
That's where your power is.

- Unknown

Day 338

A ny chance you're a control freak? I feel you. I like to be in control of my life, decisions and consequences too. Yet, it seems you have no control over what happens in life. The truth is, you don't. But you do have control over how you react to things.

Trying to control circumstances is impossible, so just focus on you. The way you view things will determine how you experience life. Take back your power!

What's happening in your life right now that you feel you have no control over?

_____

_____

How can you control or shift your response, and take back your power?

_____

_____

"The secret of change is to
focus all of your energy,
not on fighting the old, but
on building the new."

- Dan Millman

Day 339

T oday's a great day to test positive by choosing to move on, and keep moving forward. Living in the past will hold you back from experiencing the present moment and the future.

Focus your attention on what you want to change, and use your energy to intentionally build something new. Create for yourself a life that makes you feel proud and content!

If you're stuck replaying the past, what strategy can you use to get out of the loop? One of my favorite strategies is gratitude!

_____

_____

What's one thing you're ready to let go of from the past? Can you focus your attention on that today and begin building a new life?

_____

_____

"When life gets hard, try to remember the life you complain about is only a dream to some people."

- Unknown

Day 340

Most of my friends and family would agree that I'm not a complainer. Not because I'm immune to frustration, but because I practice gratitude every single day. It helps me stay focused on the good things I have in my life. Feeling thankful makes it tough to gripe about stuff.

Complaining is born our of a negative state of mind and heart. It causes physiological reactions in your body that'll harm you over time. There's so much to be grateful for, and you can test positive today by reminding yourself!

What do you complain about the most? Remember, what you think about you bring about!

_____

_____

What strategy can you use to prevent yourself from complaining?

_____

_____

"Courage doesn't always roar. Sometimes courage is the little voice at the end of the day that says I'll try again tomorrow."

- Mary Anne Radmacher

Day 341

Today's quote is a good reminder that moving past fear takes courage, even if it's done quietly and with small steps. Fear is sneaky and can take you hostage in ways you don't even realize.

Is there a person in your life that you feel you have to "walk on eggshells" around for fear of their reaction? Take back your power and be true to you! Did things not go how you thought they would, and now you're hesitant to try again? You didn't fail, you learned, so try again!

How can you overcome fear of other people's behaviors that make you feel like you have to walk on egg shells?

_____

_____

What fears are are holding you captive? Can you let them go?

_____

_____

"You are not a failure. You are in the process of finding your way to success."

- Unknown

Day 342

I f you aren't where you would like to be in your life, does that make you a failure? Why would you think that or tell yourself that? No one has ever been inspired by feeling like a failure, so please accept this fact: YOU are not a failure.

Take a deep breath and look at what you've already accomplished in your life. There may have been setbacks but take stock of your successes and how far you've come. You are enough!

Which of your accomplishments makes you feel really proud?

_____

_____

Can you set yourself up for success with whatever you're working on right now? How can you do that?

_____

_____

"Life is a series of
thousands of tiny miracles.
Notice them."

- Roald Dahl

Day 343

Test positive today by focusing your thoughts on everything that's going well, everything you have, and the people you love. When you think about all of that, isn't it miraculous? So many beautiful things, people, and experiences to notice.

If you get stuck thinking only about what you haven't achieved, or what's wrong in life, you're harming yourself in at least two ways; physiologically and psychologically. Plus, you will keep attracting more of the same!

Gratitude is a currency. When you start looking for the miracles in life, you'll find they're everywhere and you'll attract even more.

What are some things, people, or experiences, in your life that you are most grateful for?

_____

_____

Why are you grateful for these things, people, or experiences? Be specific.

_____

_____

"Everyone wants to be the sun to brighten someone's life, but why not be the moon to shine on someone's darkest hour?"

- Unknown

Day 344

Test positive today by choosing to be there for someone else. Now, you might be thinking, "Hey, wait a minute. I need support right now. I don't have anything left to give anyone else."

Here's the thing, even when you are going through difficult times, being there for someone else can help remind you of your own value. During some of the darkest hours of my life, being able to love and support someone else has given me a break from my own suffering and has helped me feel like I have a purpose. Reach out to someone in need, and you just might be the help they've been praying or hoping for.

Who can you reach out to today?

_____

_____

The next time you're struggling, how can ask for help and support? We feel good when we provide that for others, why not give someone the opportunity to feel good by providing that for you!

_____

_____

"You can't change what you did before, but you can change what you do next."

- Unknown

Day 345

The beautiful thing about looking back is that if you have the courage, you can see your part in the things that didn't go well. That's what growth is all about, learning from the past and working towards becoming better.

Good things can come from tough times, and the key is to focus on the future and how you want it to be different. Getting stuck in the past does not allow you to learn from it.

Looking back, can you see your part in things that didn't go well? What will you do differently in the future?

_____

_____

Think back to a difficult time that brought you incredible growth. In what way did you grow?

_____

_____

"Walking away from your own negative thoughts is real courage."

- Sangeeta Rana

Day 346

According to the National Science Foundation, the average person has about 12,000 to 60,000 thoughts per day. Of those, 80% are negative and 95% of those are on repeat.

Negative thoughts can lead to inflammation in your body, and fuel the stress response which also causes harm. It's equally unhealthy to bury or suppress negative thoughts. For the sake of your health, they must be dealt with and then released!

How many of your repeating negative thoughts relate to the past? Thinking about the past, which can't be changed, is a huge energy expenditure and an exercise in futility.

_____

_____

Here's a strategy to deal with people who tend to be negative about everything. When they start ranting, ask them to tell you something good about the experience they're upset about. What effect do you feel this will have?

_____

_____

"Listen and silent are spelled with the same letters. Think about it."

- Unknown

Day 347

L istening is an art, and sometimes a challenge for people like me who love to talk. Can you relate? I learned long ago that **listening** is a beautiful way to let someone know you care.

Test positive by listening more, but don't listen to respond, listen to understand. It's so important to let people know you get it, or that you wish to understand. Thats the kind of empathy that heals!

Today, practice your listening skills. Challenge yourself not to say anything but only use body language like head nodding, leaning in and making eye contact. How will this affect your interactions?

_____

_____

If you find yourself in conversation with someone who's listening to respond, not to understand, can you gently draw their attention to that? Let them know you don't need necessarily need for them to respond, you just need them to listen.

_____

_____

"We must find time to stop and thank the people who make a difference in our lives."

- John F. Kennedy

Day 348

Test positive by expressing gratitude and appreciation to the people around you today. This should actually be a regular practice and I've certainly made it one in my life. Imagine how wonderful it feels to hear these words genuinely expressed, "Thank you. I love you. I appreciate what you did for me."

When these words are spoken from the heart, they have the power to take someone from a dark place to a one of peace, happiness, and joy. The people you love will feel exactly that when you express your gratitude.

For the next week, focus on being generous with statements of gratitude and appreciation to those around you. How does doing this for others affects you?

_____

_____

The next time you get good service from a retail shop, restaurant, or service business, seek out a manager to commend an employee. What was the reaction of the manager?

_____

_____

"No one can stop you once
you have decided to grow."

- Sangeeta Rana

Day 349

If you are not living your best life right now, what's stopping you? **Who** is stopping you? As a professional coach, I see that people will often blame others for not growing in the way they want. It's the husband who says, "I can't lose weight because my wife keeps making cookies." It's the employee who says, "I can't get a promotion because my coworker doesn't like me." Are these excuses valid? Are they truly barriers?

While outside factors may influence us, the hard truth is that we're usually the primary obstacle to our own growth. We must get out of our own way, and accept full responsibility for our lives. Things that seem like barriers will completely disappear once you make a decision to move forward. Don't allow anyone stop you, not even you!

Have you been blaming something or someone for lack of forward movement or growth? Be honest with yourself, what are the real barriers?

_____

_____

What strategy can you use to get out of your own way? How can you take a step towards moving forward, towards your best life?

_____

_____

"The highest form of forgiveness is the authentic recognition that everything served and there is nothing to forgive."

- Dr. Nima Rahmany

Day 350

L etting go of negative emotions such as resentment, shame, anger, and guilt, doesn't just deliver emotional freedom, it also brings freedom from physical symptoms and illnesses that they can cause. Remember, your issues live in your tissues.

When someone has done you wrong, the goal isn't to give them a free pass for their bad behavior, but to recognize they have served a purpose. If you look back on past situations, you will recognize your own growth because of what happened with that person. Silently thank them, in your heart, for the role they played in your growth. There'll be a direct impact on your well-being if you can.

Is there someone who treated you badly that you need to forgive? Forgiveness isn't for them, it's for you. How did the situation with that person prompt your growth?

_____

_____

When negative emotions arise, what strategy can you use to release the energy so your issues won't live in your tissues?

_____

_____

"You may not always see the results of your kindness, but every bit of positive energy you contribute to the world makes it a better place for all of us."

- Lisa Currie

Day 351

T est positive with the magic of the ripple effect! Because you may not see an immediate result from your acts of kindness, it's easy to think they don't make a difference. But I challenge you to try this experiment: Starting today, and or the next four or five days, focus on small acts of kindness at your workplace, in your family, and with interactions with total strangers. Do that for several days and see what happens!

I can guarantee one or all of the following will happen:

• You will feel amazing.
• You will see the affect in other people's moods.
• You will become the **recipient** of acts of kindness because you'll be attracting them!

What random act of kindness can you perform today? Be intentional about this!

_____

_____

What strategy will you use if a recipient of your random act of kindness, does not show appreciation? For example, if you hold the door for someone and they do not say thank you, how will you deal with this?

_____

_____

"In my life, I've lived, I've loved, I've lost, I've missed, I've hurt, I've trusted, I've made mistakes, but most of all, I've learned."

- Unknown

Day 352

Test positive today by focusing your attention on all that you are, and all you've become. You can look at the past with regret if you choose, but what's the point of that? The past is over and what matters now is how you've grown along the way. If you open your mind and heart, you'll see everything that has happened pushed and pulled you into growth—sometimes kicking and screaming!

Celebrate your hard-earned wisdom today!

What are some things from the past you regret, but can now see the good that came out of it?

_____

_____

What bad experience from the past turned out to be a good thing and why? Example: marriage to an abusive partner that ended in divorce, but eventually led you to the best partner you ever imagined!

_____

_____

"Be proud of yourself for
how hard you are trying."

- Unknown

Day 353

I f you grew up like I did, you never talked about being proud of yourself. It was considered boasting, arrogant, or being full of ego. Today, we know different.

Self-love is critical to your well-being. It's where you fully accept yourself for who you are. That includes being proud of everything you've accomplished and all that you have survived!

CHOOSE to be proud of you!

What accomplishment are you most proud of from the past year? How have you celebrated this?

_____

_____

For every self-critical thought that pops into your head, can you counter it with something you're proud of yourself for doing?

_____

_____

"Being a positive person
doesn't mean you never
have negative thoughts. It
just means you don't allow
them space to take root and
grow to control your life."

- Lorri Faye

Day 354

Being positive is getting a pretty bad rap these days. Have you ever heard of "toxic positivity"? What exactly is that?! That's a rhetorical question, by the way. I suppose it could refer to living in denial, trying to wear rose-colored glasses all the time while pretending nothing ever goes wrong. Being positive about life doesn't mean you don't acknowledge the struggles; it means you remain grateful for all the good and don't allow negativity to control your life or your health.

As you know from what I shared in the beginning of this book, my daily testing positive posts on social media was my reaction to being diagnosed with breast cancer in 2020. It was my private therapy to help me stay focused on the good in my life and to stay intentional about creating more. At no point did I ever deny or suppress the fear and pain I was experiencing. Being positive while acknowledging the struggle is a superpower, not something toxic! Let's call it "curative positivity"!

What helps you stay positive during times of suffering?

_____

_____

How can you deal with negative emotions more effectively so that you can find gratitude for what is going well?

_____

_____

"Push harder than yesterday if you want a different tomorrow."

- Norm Kelly

Day 355

Test positive by getting out of your rut! Eating the same stuff every day, seeing the same people, doing the same things, even driving the same route to work—if all of these things are part of living your best life, then enjoy it! However, if you want far more out of life than what you're getting, you'll have to do something more. Your daily habits are effective predictors of what your tomorrows are going to look like. I don't mean efficient, daily habits that help you maximize time, I mean routines that have little or no meaning and are sucking the life out of you.

Being stuck in a rut is stressful and impacts quality of life. Are you willing to push a little harder to feel a little better, to experience something more, learn something new or meet someone new?

If you want your life to change, you have to change it!

Which rut can you tackle today? What can you do that's new?

_____

_____

What has kept you stuck in a rut? Dig deep and see if you can pinpoint the root cause.

_____

_____

"Never discredit your gut instinct. You are not paranoid. Your body can pick up on bad vibrations. If something deep inside of you says something is not right about a person or situation, trust it."

- Ralph Smart

Day 356

How often have you dismissed your feelings in order to do something to please someone else? Too often, we have a strong sense of what's good for us, or not good for us, and ignore it. The results are usually negative. If you allow your head to take control of every situation, you'll lose your connection with your intuition. There are times to lead with your head, but there are times you need to tune in to your gut instinct, follow its lead, and do what FEELS right.

Learn to trust your gut again!

Can you describe a time you trusted your instinct and avoided something horrible as a result?

_____

_____

Tune in to your emotional state today and ask yourself why you're feeling a certain way. Practice leaning in and listening. Write what you discovered.

_____

_____

"Connection is the energy that is created between people when they feel seen, heard, and valued– when they can give and receive without judgment."

- Brené Brown

Day 357

T est positive today by cultivating true connection. It can save lives, but it doesn't just happen. It takes real effort. You probably know people who have difficulty being a genuine friend because of conditions they place on their friendships and support. Relationships like that will never develop into a genuine connection. It begins with loving and accepting yourself, because your connection with others will never rise above your level of self-love.

Creating healthy relationships involves effort on everyone's part. Focusing on truly hearing and seeing those that you value is your responsibility and privilege. Go out and create some real connections today!

How can you show up with less judgment and competition? Ask yourself if you're putting into your relationships as much as you want to receive. Remember, you get what you give.

_____

_____

In what ways could you be a better friend?

_____

_____

"Feel free to get hugely, ridiculously happy about the tiniest little things."

- Unknown

Day 358

Isn't it so much fun to watch children get excited over literally nothing?! I just love it! How do we lose this state of joy as we get older?

Testing positive is about finding joy and happiness in the smallest of things. Positive emotions don't just happen all by themselves, you have to create that energy within yourself! It's easy to default to negativity, lack, and everything that's wrong, but the chemical soup this creates in your body is so unhealthy!

What do you feel hugely, ridiculously happy about today? If there is nothing, can you find something?

_____

_____

How can you be more intentional about joy? *Hint* It's the little things!

_____

_____

"You gotta nourish
to flourish."

- Unknown

Day 359

A re the things you're feeding yourself good for you? Think beyond food. What about the news you consume, your relationships, your physical and emotional environments? Are all of those things good for you? You can't have a positive life if you "feed" yourself negativity. If it's true, that you are what you eat, then what are you?

It's time to clean out your literal and metaphorical refrigerator and feed yourself only that which allows you to flourish.

What are you willing to clean up and clean out today in order to create a better internal and external environment?

_____

_____

Try a day of fasting this week. Fast from anything that could be harmful to your well-being. What will that be?

_____

_____

"Words kill, words give life;
they're either poison or
fruit–you choose."

- Proverbs 18:21

Day 360

How many times have you heard the phrase, "Think before you speak?" There's a really good reason for that! Words can be weapons and can stay with someone for their entire life; they can harm or heal.

A great practice is to ask yourself this question before you speak to someone, "How do I want them to respond to this?" If you have something mean and nasty to say, don't be shocked by a horrible reaction and a breach in your relationship. If you have constructive criticism, but say it with love and respect, you have a better chance of building a bridge with your communication rather than a wall.

Today, focus on how you communicate with others and think about building a bridge instead of a wall. Think about what you're going to say, and ask yourself, "Would I like someone to say the same thing to me?"

_____

_____

What aspects of your communication style do you feel could use some improvement?

_____

_____

"When you wish
good for others, good
things come back to you.
This is the law of nature."

- Sri Sri Ravi Shankar

Day 361

Wow! This is tough to do if you've been hurt, harassed, bullied, disrespected or worse! But holding on to those negative feelings and energy will hurt YOU!

It's time to let go of anger, vengefulness, and unforgiveness. Send out only what you want to come back. The energetic boomerang is a law!

What are you willing to let go of today that has been hurting you emotionally? Who needs to be forgiven, what anger needs to be let released?

_____

_____

Why have you been holding onto this for so long?

_____

_____

"Psychological invalidation is
one of the most lethal forms
of emotional abuse. It kills
confidence, creativity,
and individuality."

- Dr. Anne Brown RNMS

Day 362

H ave you ever had someone say to you, "You shouldn't feel that way," or anything to that effect? How did that make you feel? Invalidated, invisible, insignificant, stupid?

When someone shares their feelings, listen with your heart and not just your ears. Validate what you hear, and let them know that you understand, or at least you're trying to understand. Just because someone feels different than you, doesn't make them wrong. It's often just two different perspectives. Judgement or invalidation of someone's feelings puts them into the stress response. When you listen and validate without judgment, it helps the other person feel seen and allows them to safely halt their stress response. In a leadership position, or as a parent, this is even more critical. In this state, their safety becomes more at risk as well as those around them.

What questions can you ask so you can see things from the other persons perspective?

_____

_____

Don't offer advice unless you're asked. Listen to understand, not just to respond. If they're upset, ask how you can support them. Who needs this from you today?

_____

_____

"Sit with it. Sit with it. Sit with it. Sit with it. Even though you want to run. Even when it's heavy and difficult. Even though you're not quite sure of the way through. Healing happens by feeling."

- Dr. Rebecca Ray

Day 363

How can you test positive if you are feeling or experiencing pain, suffering, regret, grief, or shame? The truth is, it's impossible to be positive and truly content if you don't! Someone can be positive on the surface—smiling, acting happy, and the life of the party—but hurting on the inside.

That's the stuff you need to sit with, lean into, feel, and release! Talk about it, write about it, move it out, or your issues will live in your tissues. To be truly content is to acknowledge what is difficult and negative, work through it, and find your way back to positivity and gratitude.

How will you release negative emotions you may be experiencing today? What works for you?

_____

_____

What's your strategy for preventing the negative emotions from popping up in the first place? For example, is there someone in your life who makes you angry that you could try to spend little or no time with?

_____

_____

"What helped you over the great obstacles of life?" was asked of a highly successful man.

"The other obstacles," he replied.

- Napoleon Hill

Day 364

I'm sure you're familiar with the expression, "Life is 10% what happens to you and 90% how you react." Isn't that the truth? In every moment, and in every situation, you have a choice. If you choose to open your mind and heart to the gift that's present in every challenge, the next challenge you face will be a little easier to deal with. With each difficulty you face, you acquire wisdom, patience, and the understanding that you can get through anything.

Learn from the past, and remember that you are powerful!

What powerful lesson did you learn from a past challenge?

_____

_____

What's a strategy that gets you through difficult times, and works every time? For me, it's gratitude.

_____

_____

"When you seek beauty in all people and all things, you will not only find it, you will become it."

- Unknown

Day 365

We can be pretty quick to see what's wrong in others, our surroundings, and ourselves. Our minds work overtime trying to keep us focused on whatever is negative, but we can shift that mindset. How would things be different if you focused on all that is beautiful and right instead? How would you feel about yourself if you simply noticed your own inherent beauty, both inside and out?

There is good in everyone and everything if you choose to see it. Your day will become whatever you decide, so make it a great day!

Today, challenge your thoughts when they veer towards what's wrong. What's right, and what's good in the situation?

_____

_____

For the next seven days, stop yourself whenever you're about to make a negative comment about someone or something. How can you challenge yourself to say something positive instead and see if the week goes differently for you?

_____

_____

Acknowledgments

At the end of the day, we each have to carry our own burdens and solve our own problems, but there's nothing like having a tribe of people cheering you on, sending you love, and holding space for your every emotion. I have such a tribe. They're my people and I am their person. My life would be so empty without their presence, and I want all of them to know I'm grateful they're in my life.

My children have been a never-ending source of love, support, hope, and rock solid belief in my ability to conquer anything! My life partner, David, came into my life partway through this journey. He has taught me how to receive, and how to truly be myself. He is my safe place, and my home.

My tight-knit group of lady friends (we call ourselves the Divas) have been with me every step of the way, and not just in these last few years, but in the twenty years previous where there was much sorrow and struggle. They've also been there through the many good times. Divas, you are my soul sisters.

Keith has been my partner in this book, my mentor, advisor and cheerleader, for the last several years. This project could not have been done without him.

Mary Ann, the owner of Top Safety Speakers, is another soul sister. During the darkest times, you were there on the phone, and in many beautiful, inspirational and hope-filled messages every week. I am so grateful!

Debbie, yet another soul sister, and my body talk therapist. You've cleared so many energetic blockages that freed me up to live a life filled with health, joy, happiness and surrender. I am living my best life, thanks to all the work we have done together.

I am filled with gratitude for my family, extended family and my family of choice. You all know who you are, and your belief in me is my jet fuel.

Special thanks to Steve Heibert, of Personal Expressions Photography, for the incredible photograph that became the cover of this book. You are a true artist and capture the beauty of our province so incredibly.

Sean Ferstl, many thanks for the fabulous and creative work on the beautiful cover of this devotional.

To my clients, social media connections, and the beautiful people who I've had the privilege to support in their journeys—thank you for supporting me and mine! All the beautiful messages I've received during the two years of doing daily testing positive posts, have filled my heart in indescribable ways. We're here to walk each other home and I recognize that my role is not to take your suffering from you, but rather to walk with you so that you are not alone in your struggle. You've done that for me by loving these posts, and expressing your gratitude to me. I love you all so very much, and I'm privileged to walk this planet with you at this time.

Manufactured by Amazon.ca
Acheson, AB

15034039R00418